sew cute Baby Animals

Mix & Match 17 Paper-Pieced Blocks
6 Nursery Projects

Mary Hertel

C&T PUBLISHING

Text copyright © 2022 by Mary Hertel

Photography and artwork copyright © 2022 by C&T Publishing, Inc.

Publisher: Amy Barrett-Daffin

Creative Director: Gailen Runge

Acquisitions Editor: Roxane Cerda

Managing Editor: Liz Aneloski

Editor: Katie Van Amburg

Technical Editor: Julie Waldman

Cover/Book Designer: April Mostek

Production Coordinator: Tim Manibusan

Production Editor: Alice Mace Nakanishi

Illustrator: Aliza Shalit

Photography Assistant: Gabriel Martinez

Photography by Lauren Herberg of C&T Publishing, Inc., unless otherwise noted

Published by C&T Publishing, Inc., P.O. Box 1456, Lafayette, CA 94549

Library of Congress Cataloging-in-Publication Data

Names: Hertel, Mary, 1955- author.

Title: Sew cute baby animals : mix & match 17 paper-pieced blocks 6 nursery projects / Mary Hertel.

Description: Lafayette : C&T Publishing, 2022.

Identifiers: LCCN 2021042194 | ISBN 9781644031452 (trade paperback) | ISBN 9781644031469 (ebook)

Subjects: LCSH: Patchwork--Patterns. | Children's quilts. | Animals in art.

Classification: LCC TT835 .H44693 2022 | DDC 746.46/041--dc23

LC record available at https://lccn.loc.gov/2021042194

Printed in the USA

10 9 8 7 6 5 4 3 2 1

Dedication I dedicate this book to my patrons, who are always motivating me to keep creating books and patterns. Your support means so much to me and your suggestions are always appreciated.

Acknowledgments Thank you to the many quilt shop owners around the world who carry my patterns and books. Having my patterns in your store is an honor. At one time, I worked in a quilt shop, so I know how hard you work to offer quality fabric and supplies to your patrons.

Contents

PROJECTS   12

Introduction

Oh, baby—better get ready for cuteness overload!

This book is filled with everything **baby**: quilted blankets, bibs, burp cloths, diaper totes, and some of the sweetest baby animal patterns ever! If there is a baby or toddler in your life—or will be in the future—this is the book for you. You will find the cutest baby animal blocks to add to your projects, from pets and farm animals like a calf, kitten, chick, puppy, and foal to wild animals like a baby sloth, panda cub, baby zebra, and baby penguin.

This book includes step-by-step instructions for paper piecing (see Paper-Piecing Basics, next page), six fun baby projects, and seventeen adorable baby animal block patterns. Some of the blocks are 8″ × 8″ squares, and some are a combination of two square blocks 8″ × 8″ sewn together, which result in a rectangular block that is 8″ × 15½″.

As in my previous books, all the block patterns are interchangeable in all the projects. That means you can conceivably create loads of projects using my book. Plus, these blocks will also fit into the projects from my previous five books, which means you can be super-creative! You don't have to use these animal blocks only for baby projects. I can't wait to make a sloth quilt for my sofa. Who doesn't love a sloth?

Let's get to the fun and start paper piecing these adorable blocks. Everything you need to know is right here!

Photo by Gail Cameron

Paper-Piecing Basics

Paper piecing is a simple, straightforward method of sewing a design into a project. Perhaps you have experienced the joy and satisfaction of seeing the finished image after adding the last piece to a jigsaw puzzle. The effects of paper piecing are no different. Anyone with basic sewing skills can master paper piecing, as the approach used in all my previous books (which are tailored for beginners) and this book is essentially sewing by number. Paper piecing is also a creative means of using up oddly shaped pieces of fabric that might otherwise have been relegated to the scrap pile.

Tools

- Paper (I recommend Carol Doak's Foundation Paper by C&T Publishing.)

- Sharp scissors

- Rotary cutter and mat

- Ruler with an easy-to-read ¼″ line (such as Add-a-Quarter ruler by CM Designs)

- Multiuse tool (such as Alex Anderson's 4-in-1 Essential Sewing Tool by C&T Publishing) or seam ripper

- Flat-head straight pins

- Lamp or natural light source

- Sewing machine

- Iron and pressing board

Things to Know

STITCH LENGTH

Set the stitch length at 1.5, which is about 20 stitches per inch. When paper piecing, the stitch perforations must be close together to allow the paper to tear easily, but not so close that ripping out a seam is an impossible task.

PREPARE A CONVENIENT WORK STATION

Have the iron, pressing board, and cutting mat close to the sewing machine. There should be a light source handy for positioning scrap pieces on the back of the block. A window works well during the day and a lamp at night.

THE BUTTERFLY EFFECT

After sewing a seamline, the fabric is flipped behind the numbered piece that you are currently attaching. This creates a butterfly effect, meaning that the fabric scrap needs to be lined up to the seam in such a way that it will cover the space you are sewing after it is flipped into place. If you are concerned that the size of the scrap is insufficient, pin along the seamline and try flipping the scrap into place before sewing the seam. That way, if the scrap does not cover the area sufficiently, you can adjust it or find a larger scrap.

FOLLOW ALONG

If you are new to paper piecing, follow along for practice using the Baby Sloth block, Part 1 (page 50) and Part 2 (page 51), as you read the following instructions.

Preparing the Patterns

1 Make the recommended number of color copies of the original block. (You need 3 copies for the Baby Sloth, Part 1 block.)

2 Cut the block into the segments denoted by the capital letters in circles, *adding ¼″ seam allowances along the red lines and the outside edges of the block.* For the example, use 1 copy for Segments A and C, 1 copy for Segments D and E, and 1 copy for Segment B.

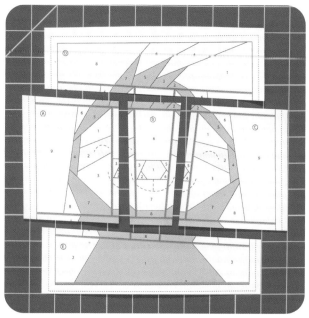

Segments A, B, C, D, and E with ¼″ seam allowances around outside edges

Paper Piecing a Segment

Always stitch pieces in numerical order. Don't forget to set your stitch length (page 7) to 1.5, or about 20 stitches per inch.

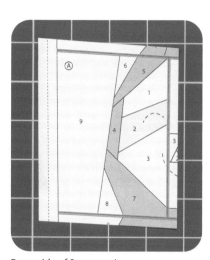

Front side of Segment A

1 Pin the *wrong* side of the Piece 1 fabric onto the *unprinted* side of the paper pattern. The right side of the fabric faces you (away from the paper).

2 Bend the paper pattern along the seamline between Pieces 1 and 2. Use the side of a pencil or a pressing tool (such as the presser cap on Alex Anderson's 4-in-1 Essential Sewing Tool) and a heavy piece of tagboard (such as a bookmark or postcard) to make the fold. (This will help you align the fabric for Piece 2.)

3 Use the Add-a-Quarter ruler to trim the fabric behind Piece 1 to ¼".

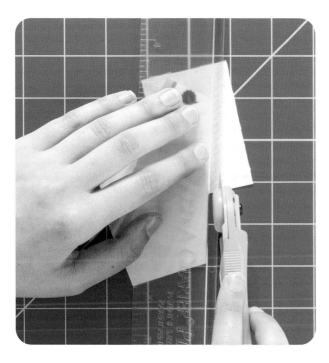

4 Keeping the pattern bent back along the seamline, align the Piece 2 fabric with the fabric from Piece 1, right sides together. The fabric for Piece 2 will be flipped into place after sewing. Pin in place.

Tip: Right Sides Together   *As you are piecing, the right sides of fabric should always be together.*

5 Flip the pattern flat and sew ¼" beyond the seamline at the beginning and the end of this seam (as shown by the green line). No backtacking is needed, as the ends of the seams will be stitched over by other seams. Notice that the fabric for Piece 2 is much larger than needed; it will be trimmed later.

Tip: Double-Check to Avoid Seam Ripping

I like to use large scraps (but no larger than 9" × 11") and trim the piece after sewing it in place. As you place the fabric under your presser foot to sew, the seam allowance and the shape you are filling should be to your right. The shape you previously completed should be to your left. Before sewing, do a mental check. Ask yourself these two questions: "Is the piece I am working on to my right?" and "Is the majority of my fabric to my left?" If the answer is yes, then sew. This simple check will eliminate much seam ripping.

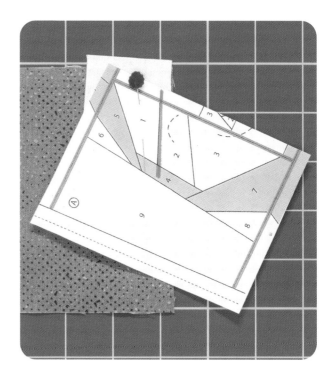

6 Flip the fabric into position behind Piece 2 and press. Pin it in place to keep it flat.

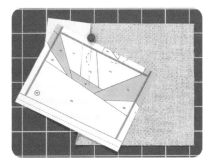

7 Trim the fabric a generous ½″ beyond the first and second edge of Piece 2 (see the dotted lines). *Do not cut the pattern.*

Trimming first side of Piece 2

Trimming second side of Piece 2

8 Continue to add the remaining pieces in the same manner as you added Piece 2.

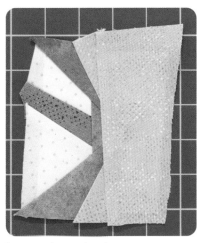

Segment A completed

Tip: Stitches Interfering?

Overstitching the seams may at times interfere with an exact fold along a stitching line. In this case, tear the paper just enough to release it from the stitching.

9 Trim the seam allowance of Segment A to an *exact* ¼″ seam, using a rotary cutter, a mat, and a ruler with a ¼″ line.

The segment is now ready to be sewn to the other segments. Follow the same process to make Segments B, C, D, and E.

Joining Segments

Note: Make sure each segment is trimmed so that it has an exact ¼″ seam allowance along the red segment seamline only. Do not trim the outer edge seam allowances at this time.

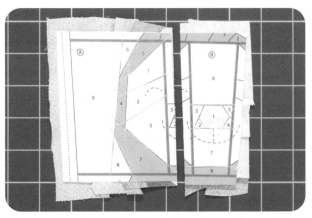

Segments have ¼″ seam allowances where they will be joined.

1 With right sides together, pin together the edges of Segments A and B, matching the red sewing lines. Push a straight pin through the end of each red line to help align them as closely as possible. Sew on the red line and ¼″ past the red line on both ends.

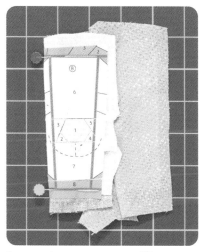

Sew together segments on red line.

2 Remove the paper from the seam allowance *only* to eliminate the possibility of the paper getting trapped under the seams.

3 Press the seam to a side. Let the seam "show" you in which direction it wants to be pressed.

Continue joining segments until Baby Sloth, Part 1, is complete. Repeat the process of paper-piecing, beginning with Preparing the Patterns (page 8) for Baby Sloth, Part 2.

Joining Blocks

Blue lines join completed blocks. Unlike red segment seams, blue-line seams are backtacked at the beginning and end.

1 Trim only the edges on Part 1 and Part 2 that have a *blue* line. Trim these edges ¼″ away from the blue line.

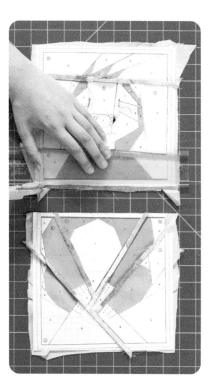

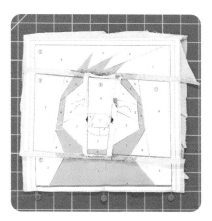

2 Pin the Part 1 and the Part 2 block with right sides together, matching the blue lines.

3 Sew on the blue line, backtacking at the beginning and end of the seam. Rip the paper from the seam area. Press the block open.

Tip: Finish Before Trimming

Make sure never to trim the excess fabric from the outer edges of the block until the block is finished and joined to its partner block. After that, it is safe to square up the block using a cutting mat, ruler, and rotary cutter. A rectangular block should measure 8″ × 15½″ unfinished.

4 Complete any embroidery *while the paper is still attached.* The paper acts as a stabilizer and will keep the block from stretching. *After the block has been attached to the project, the paper may be removed.*

Baby Quilt

FINISHED QUILT: 38½˝ × 35½˝

Use any baby animals of your choice to create a custom quilt for your toddler.

Materials

Fabric A: ⅜ yard for first sashing

Fabric B: ⅓ yard for second sashing

Fabric C: ¾ yard for border and binding

Fabric D: 1½ yard for backing

Fabric E: 1 yard background fabric for paper-pieced blocks

Assorted scraps: For paper piecing (See your selected block's materials list.)

Batting: 1 rectangle 44″ × 47″

Cutting

WOF = width of fabric

Fabric A

Fold fabric selvage to selvage.

- Cut 7 strips 1½″ × WOF. Subcut into:

  4 rectangles 1½″ × 17½″

  8 rectangles 1½″ × 10″

  14 rectangles 1½″ × 8″

  2 rectangles 1½″ × 6½″

Fabric B

Fold fabric selvage to selvage.

- Cut 7 strips 1½″ × WOF. Subcut into 4 rectangles 1½″ × 10″.

- Set remaining 6 strips aside for the time being.

Fabric C

Fold fabric selvage to selvage.

- Cut 4 strips 3½″ × WOF for border.

- Cut 4 strips 2½″ × WOF for binding.

Fabric E

- Cut 1 rectangle 4½″ × 8″.

- Use remaining Fabric E for paper piecing background of blocks.

Sewing

Use ¼″ seams throughout, unless otherwise directed.

PAPER-PIECED BLOCKS

Refer to Paper-Piecing Basics (page 7) as needed. Refer to Block Patterns (page 39) to choose blocks.

1 Paper piece 4 selected *square* blocks, using Fabric E as the background fabric of each block and the assorted scraps for the rest of the block.

2 Paper piece 2 selected *vertical rectangular* blocks, using Fabric E as the background fabric of each block and the assorted scraps for the rest of the block.

3 Add any necessary embroidery.

4 Trim each square block to 8″ × 8″. Trim each rectangular block to 8″ × 15½″.

ATTACH THE FIRST SASHINGS TO THE BLOCKS

1 Sew a Fabric A 1½″ × 8″ strip to the top and bottom of each square and rectangular block, and to the top and bottom of the 4½″ × 8″ rectangle. Press the seams toward the sashing.

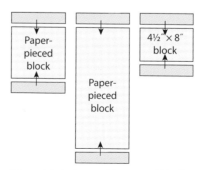

Sew a strip to top and bottom of blocks.

2 Sew a Fabric A 1½" × 10" strip to the sides of the square blocks. Press the seams toward the sashing.

Sew strips to side edges of square blocks.

3 Sew a Fabric A 1½" × 15½" strip to the sides of the rectangular blocks. Press the seams toward the sashing.

4 Sew a Fabric A 1½" × 6½" strip to the sides of the 4½" × 8" rectangle. Press the seams toward the sashing.

ATTACH THE SECOND SASHINGS TO THE BLOCKS

Note: The rows run vertically.

1 **Row 1:** Sew a Fabric B 1½" × 10" strip to connect a square block to a rectangular block, placing the square block at the top of the row. Press the seams toward the sashing.

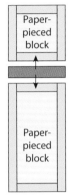

Connect square block and rectangular block for Row 1.

2 **Row 2:** Sew 2 Fabric B 1½" × 10" strips to connect a square block, the center rectangle, and a second square block. Press the seams toward the sashing.

3 **Row 3:** Sew a Fabric B 1½" × 10" strip to connect a rectangular block to a square block, placing the rectangular block at the top. Press the seams toward the sashing.

ASSEMBLE THE ROWS WITH SASHING

1 Sew a Fabric B 1½" × WOF strip to each side edge of Row 1, and to the right sides of Row 2 and Row 3. Press the seams toward the sashing. Trim away any excess fabric from strips.

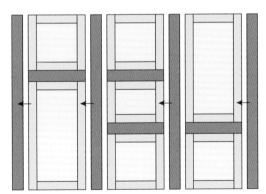

Sew second sashing to sides of rows.

2 Sew the 3 rows together.

3 Sew a Fabric B 1½" × WOF sashing strip to the top and bottom of the quilt. Press the seams toward the sashing. Trim away any excess fabric from the strips.

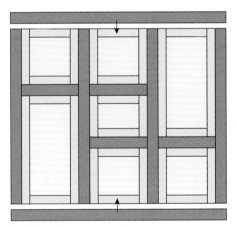

Sashing strips at top and bottom

ATTACH THE BORDER

1 Sew a Fabric C 3½″ × WOF strip to the top and bottom of the quilt. Press the seams toward the border. Trim any excess fabric from the sides of the strips.

2 Sew a Fabric C 3½″ × WOF strip to the sides of the quilt. Press the seams toward the border. Trim any excess fabric from the sides of the strips.

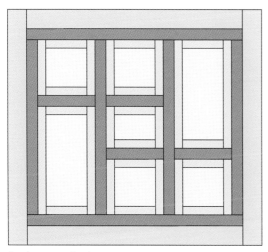

Borders sewn in place

QUILTING

1 Remove the paper from the back of the paper-pieced blocks.

2 Layer the Fabric D backing (right side facing down), batting, and quilt top (right side facing up).

3 Pin all 3 layers together and quilt as desired.

BINDING

1 Pin together 2 Fabric C 2½″ × WOF binding strips, overlapping on a right (90°) angle, with right sides together. Mark a diagonal line from Corner A to Corner B. Sew on the diagonal line to connect the strips. Trim the seam to ¼″. Continue, adding the rest of the 4 Fabric C strips together in this manner to make 1 long, continuous strip.

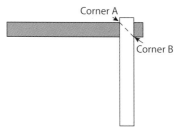

Strips overlap at right angle. Mark and sew on diagonal line.

2 Press the WOF strips in half lengthwise with the wrong sides together.

3 Align the raw edges of the binding strip with the raw edges of the quilt. Bend the beginning of the strip on a right (90°) angle with the tail facing away from the quilt.

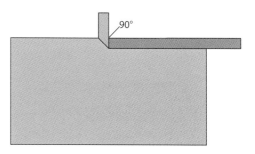

4 Stitch ¼″ from the raw edges. Stop stitching ¼″ from the first corner and backtack.

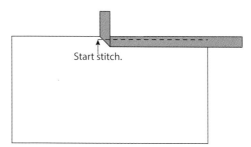

Pin binding strip to quilt and start stitching here.

5 Fold the binding strip straight up. The raw edge of the binding strip should align with the raw edge of the second side of the quilt.

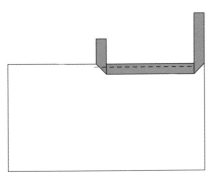

Starting first corner

6 Fold the binding strip straight down to overlap the second edge of the quilt. Start stitching at the top corner and continue until ¼″ from the next corner and backtack.

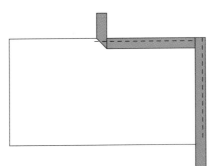

Finishing first corner

7 Continue in this manner around the remaining sides of the quilt, back-tacking and turning at each corner.

8 Trim the end of the binding strip so it overlaps the angled beginning section by 2″. Trim away the remaining tail.

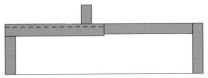

Overlap binding tails.

9 Press the binding around to the back of the quilt and hand stitch in place, easing in the fullness where the tails overlap.

· French Knot ·

When making the paper-pieced blocks in this book, you will often use the French knot embroidery stitch. Follow the instructions below to make French knots when directed.

Use 6 strands of floss and a tapestry needle. Thread the needle with no more than 18″ of floss and tie a knot at one end.

1 Pull the floss from the back to the front of the block, so the knot will be on the back. Wrap the floss around the tip of the needle twice.

spot where the floss first came through the fabric.

3 Gently pull the floss through the wraps and to the back of the block. Knot and cut the floss.

2 Poke the needle back into the block from the front to the back, poking a hole very close to the

Cozy Baby Quilt

FINISHED QUILT: 34½″ × 34½″

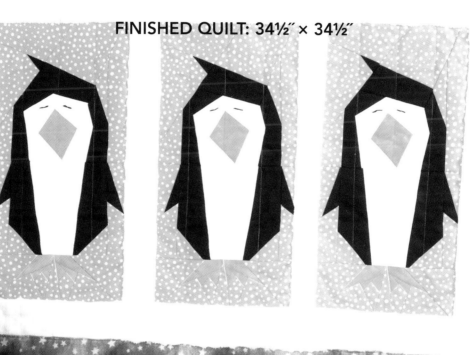

Materials

Fabric A: ⅔ yard for minky fabric

Fabric B: ½ yard for paper piecing background

Fabric C: 40″ × 40″ square of flannel for backing

Assorted scraps: For paper piecing (See your selected block's materials list.)

Fusible fleece: 30″ × 30″ square (such as Pellon 987F)

Cutting

WOF = width of fabric. Fold fabric selvage to selvage.

Fabric A

• Cut 2 strips 2½″ × WOF. Subcut into 2 pieces 2½″ × 15½″ from 1 WOF strip; save the second WOF strip for later.

• Cut 1 strip 2″ × WOF. Subcut into 2 pieces 2″ × 15½″.

• Cut 1 rectangle 13″ × 30″.

Sewing

Use ¼″ seams throughout, unless otherwise directed.

PAPER-PIECED BLOCKS

Refer to Paper-Piecing Basics (page 7) as needed. Refer to Block Patterns (page 39) to choose blocks.

1 Paper piece 3 selected rectangular blocks, using Fabric B as the background fabric of each block and the assorted scraps for the rest of the block.

2 Trim each block to 8″ × 15½″.

ATTACH THE SASHING TO THE BLOCKS

1 Sew a Fabric A 2″ × 15½″ strip to each long side of 1 paper-pieced block. Press the seams toward the sashing strips.

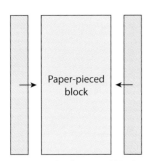

Sew strips to 2 sides of block.

2 Sew a paper-pieced block to each long side of the paper-pieced unit. Press the seams toward the sashing strips.

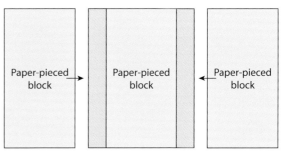

Sew block to each side.

3 Sew a Fabric A 2½″ × 15½″ strip to each side of the paper-pieced block unit. Press the seam toward the sashing strip.

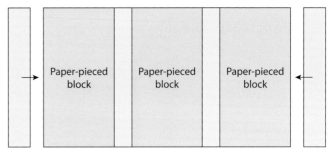

Sew strips to sides of block unit.

4 Sew a Fabric A 13″ × 30″ strip to the top of the paper-pieced block unit. Press the seam toward the minky fabric.

5 Sew a Fabric A 2½″ × 30″ strip to the bottom of the paper-pieced blocks. Press the seam toward the minky fabric.

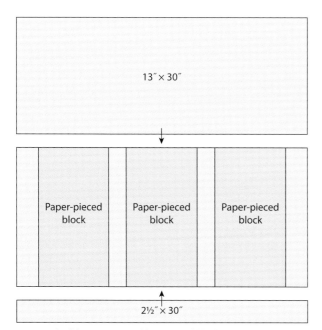

Sew minky fabric to top and bottom of blocks.

6 Remove the paper from the back of the paper-pieced blocks.

7 Steam press the 30″ × 30″ square of fusible fleece to the back of the paper-pieced unit.

ADD BACKING

1 Fold each side of the 40″ × 40″ flannel square in half and place a pin to mark the center of each side.

2 Fold each side of the 30″ × 30″ paper-pieced unit in half and place a pin to mark the center of each side.

3 With right sides together, pin the 30″ × 30″ rectangle to the 40″ × 40″ flannel, matching the center marks. There will be extra backing fabric at each corner.

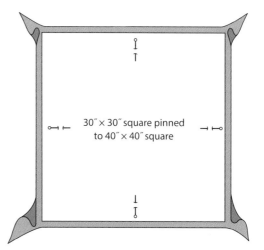

Front of quilt pinned to back of quilt

4 Sew together the top edge and the 2 sides separately, starting and stopping ¼″ from the end of each corner, and backtacking.

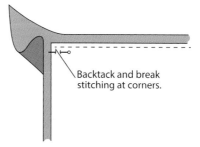

Backtack ¼″ from beginning and end of each seam.

5 Sew the bottom edge the same way, leaving an 8″ opening in the center, for turning. *Do not* turn right side out at this time.

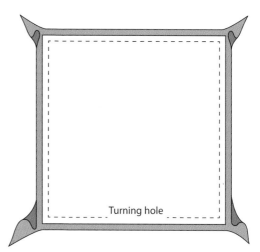

Leave turning hole in center of bottom seam.

SEW THE MITERED CORNERS

1 Flatten a corner of the quilt by folding the quilt top in half diagonally from corner to corner. Also flatten the flannel fabric that extends past the edges of the quilt top, right sides together, approximately 3″ on each side.

2 Pin the flannel corners together, keeping the quilt folded on an angle. Sew together, backtacking ¼″ from the edge where it meets the minky fabric. Trim any excess fabric.

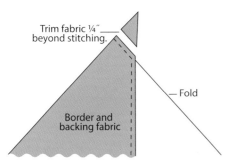

Flatten corner of quilt at 45° angle, and sew.

3 Repeat Steps 1 and 2 for the remaining 3 corners.

4 Turn the quilt right side out through the turning hole. Use a tool (such as Alex Anderson's 4-in 1 Essential Sewing Tool by C&T Publishing) to poke the corners of the quilt square.

5 Stitch the turning hole closed.

QUILT

1 Press the outer borders and corners of the quilt flat.

2 Quilt as desired, sewing through all layers.

Diaper Tote

FINISHED TOTE: 17″ wide × 11½″ high × 4 deep

"In came the doctor, in came the nurse, in came the lady with the alligator purse!"
This amazing diaper tote has lots of inside pockets. With its adjustable straps, it
can be carried as a messenger tote or attached directly to the baby's stroller.

Materials

Fabric A: 1¼ yards for main fabric

Fabric B: 2 yards for lining, sashing, pockets, and sleeve

Fabric C: Fat eighth (9″ × 21″) for paper piecing background

Assorted scraps: For paper piecing (See your selected block's materials list.)

One-sided fusible foam stabilizer: 21½″ × 28½″ rectangle (such as Bosal In-R-Form Single Sided Fusible Foam Stabilizer)

Fusible fleece: ½ yard (such as Pellon 987F Fusible Fleece)

Fusible interfacing (45″ wide): 1⅛ yards (I recommend Pellon 809 Décor-Bond.)

Heavy-duty snaps: 8

Foam board: 3½″ × 16½″ rectangle for sleeve

Cutting

WOF = width of fabric. Fold fabric selvage to selvage.

Fabric A

- Cut 4 strips 3½″ × WOF. Subcut 2 strips into 4 rectangles 3½″ × 11″. Set other 2 strips aside for later.
- Cut 1 rectangle 21½″ × 28½″.
- Cut 1 rectangle 4″ × 17½″.

Fabric B

- Cut 2 strips 1½″ × WOF. Subcut into 2 rectangles 1½″ × 8″ and 2 rectangles 1½″ × 17½″ for flap sashing.
- Cut 1 rectangle 21½″ × 28½″ for lining.
- Cut 1 rectangle 13½″ × 17½″ for flap lining.
- Cut 4 rectangles 8″ × 17″ for pockets.
- Cut 2 strips 4½″ × 21″ for sleeve.

Fabric C

- *For square block layout only:* Cut 2 rectangles 4″ × 8″.

Fusible fleece

- Cut 1 rectangle 13½″ × 17½″.

Fusible interfacing

- Cut 1 rectangle 21½″ × 28½″.
- Cut 2 strips 3½″ × 11″.
- Cut 1 strip 3½″ × 42″.
- Cut 2 rectangles 8″ × 17″.

Sewing

Use ¼″ seams throughout, unless otherwise directed.

PAPER-PIECED BLOCKS

Refer to Paper-Piecing Basics (page 7) as needed. Refer to Block Patterns (page 39) to choose a block.

1 Paper piece 1 selected *horizontal rectangular* block, or 1 *square* block, using Fabric C as the background fabric of the block and the assorted scraps for the rest of the block.

2 Add any necessary embroidery.

3 Trim the block to 8″ × 15½″. If using an 8″ × 8″ square block, trim to 8″ × 8″ and then sew a 4″ × 8″ rectangle of Fabric C to each side of the square block, which will make it comparable to an 8″ × 15½″ rectangular block.

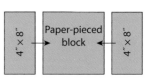

If using 8″ × 8″ square block, sew 4″ × 8″ rectangle of Fabric C to each side.

ATTACH THE SASHING TO THE BLOCK

1 Sew a Fabric B 1½″ × 8″ strip to the sides of the paper-pieced block. Press the seams toward the sashing strips.

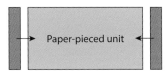

Sew strip to each side of block.

2 Sew a Fabric B 1½″ × 17½″ strip to the top and bottom of the paper-pieced block. Press the seam toward the sashing strip.

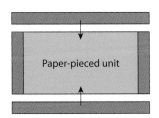

Sew strip to top and bottom of block.

3 Sew a Fabric A 4″ × 17½″ strip to the top of the paper-pieced unit. Press the seams toward the sashing strips.

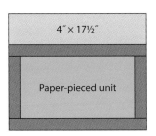

Sew main fabric strip to top of unit.

CREATE THE FLAP AND QUILT

1 Remove the paper from the back of the paper-pieced block.

2 Press the 13½″ × 17½″ fusible fleece to the back of the paper-pieced unit.

3 With right sides together, pin a Fabric B 13½″ × 17½″ rectangle over the paper-pieced unit. Sew together along the sides and bottom only, leaving the top open. Turn the flap right sides out and press. Topstitch ¼″ away from the 3 stitched edges.

4 Quilt the flap as desired, quilting through all layers.

POCKETS

1 Press a piece of fusible interfacing to the back of 2 Fabric B 8″ × 17″ rectangles.

2 With right sides together, pin the remaining 2 Fabric B 8″ × 17″ rectangles to the pockets. Sew around all sides, leaving a 5″ turning hole at the bottom of each pocket.

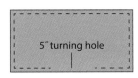

3 Turn each pocket right side out and press.

4 Press the 21½″ × 28½″ piece of fusible interfacing to the back of the Fabric B 21½″ × 28½″ lining.

5 Place each pocket as shown, pinning the pockets to the right side of the Fabric B 21½″ × 28½″ lining.

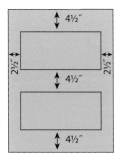

Pocket placement on lining

6 Sew around the sides and bottom of each pocket, catching the 5″ turning hole in the stitching. *Note: Leave the long edges closest to the top and bottom of the lining open.*

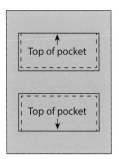

Leave these sides of pockets open.

7 Sew divisions in pockets where desired. (I suggest sewing across the pockets every 5½″, or sewing right down the middle, which will divide the pocket into 8″ sections.)

TOTE LINING WITH BOXED BOTTOM

1 With right sides together, fold the lining in half with the 21½″ edges at the top.

2 Sew a ½″ seam on the two sides of the lining. Leave a 7″ turning hole on one side. Leave the top of the bag open.

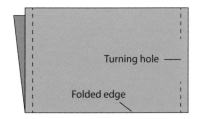

Turning hole ———

Folded edge

3 Flatten the corner of the bag so the side seam is centered in the middle. Use a ruler and a chalk pen to mark a 4″ line, making sure the 2″ mark is on the seamline. Sew on this line.

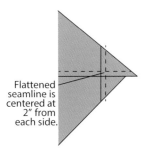

Flattened seamline is centered at 2″ from each side.

Sew box corner.

4 Trim the corner off about ½″ from the seam. Repeat for the other corner of the bag. Do not turn it right side out.

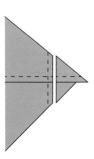

Trim corner.

TOTE BODY WITH BOXED BOTTOM

1 Press the fusible stabilizer to the wrong side of Fabric A 21½″ × 28½″. Use a steam iron and a pressing cloth for best results.

2 With right sides together, center and baste the quilted flap to a 21½″ edge of the tote body.

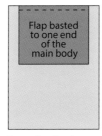

Flap basted to one end of the main body

Baste flap in place.

3 With right sides together, fold the body in half with the 21½″ edges at the top.

4 Sew a ½″ seam on the 2 sides of the bag body, making sure to catch all layers. Leave the top of the bag open.

Sew sides of tote body.

5 Repeat Tote Lining with Boxed Bottom, Steps 3 and 4 (at left), to create boxed corners for the main body of the tote. Turn the tote body right side out.

PREPARE THE TWO SHORT STRAPS

1 Press the fusible interfacing strips to the wrong sides of 2 Fabric A 3½″ × 11 strips.

2 With right sides together, sew a plain Fabric A 3½″ × 11″ strip to a matching strip with interfacing. Sew around 3 sides, leaving 1 side 3½″ open for turning. Repeat for the second short strap.

Leave one end open for turning.

Stitch 3 sides of short straps.

3 Trim the corners, then turn each strap right side out and press. Top-stitch ½″ from the 3 sewn edges.

PREPARE THE LONG STRAP

1 Press the fusible interfacing strip to the wrong side of the Fabric A 3½″ × 42 strip.

2 With right sides together, sew a plain Fabric A 3½″ × 42″ strip to the matching interfaced strip. Sew around 4 sides, leaving a 7″ opening along 1 long edge for turning.

7″ turning hole

Sew 1 long strap.

3 Trim the corners, then turn the strap right side out and press. Hand stitch the turning hole closed. Top-stitch ½″ from the 4 edges.

ASSEMBLE TOTE BODY

1 Pin the open edge of each short strap to the right side top of each side edge of the tote body, centering the side seam of the bag in the middle of the strap. Baste in place.

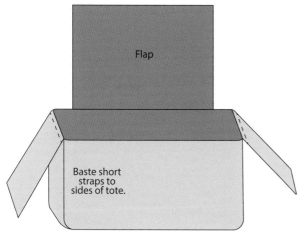

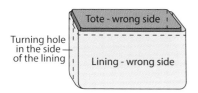

Baste short strap to each side.

2 With right sides together, slide the tote body inside the lining. Pin the top edges together, matching the side seams. The short straps and the bag flap should be in between the tote body and the lining. Using a ½″ seam, sew along the top edge, being sure to catch all edges.

3 Turn the tote right side out by gently pulling the tote body through the turning hole in the side of the lining. Hand sew the turning hole closed.

4 Tuck the lining inside the tote body and topstitch ½″ from the top edge, being careful to keep the flap and short straps free from the stitching.

ATTACH THE SNAPS

1 On each short strap, and following the manufacturer's directions, attach 2 male snaps to the side closest to the tote, and 2 female snaps on the opposite edge.

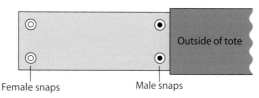

Placement of snaps on short straps

2 On the long strap, attach 2 female snaps 1″ from each end, and 2 male snaps approximately 8″ from the female snaps. Line up the placement of these snaps with the snaps on the short straps.

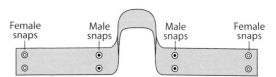

Placement of snaps on long strap

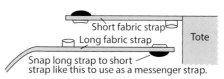

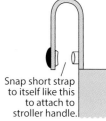

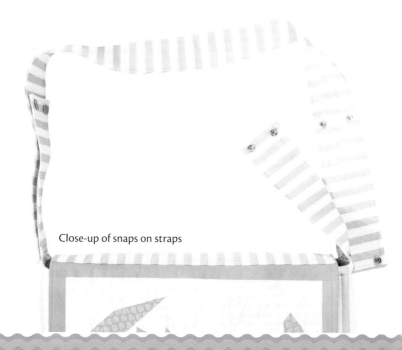

Close-up of snaps on straps

SLEEVE

1 Hem 1 short end of each Fabric B 4½″ × 21″ rectangle by pressing under ½″, then press under another ½″. Stitch ⅜″ from each end.

2 Place the 2 strips right sides together and sew around the 3 unhemmed edges of the sleeve.

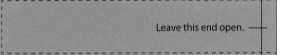

Leave this end open.

Sew 3 sides of sleeve.

3 Turn sleeve right side out and slide the 3½″ × 16½″ foam board into the sleeve. Fold the excess under the sleeve and place the sleeve on the inside, at the bottom of the bag. (The foam board can be easily removed when laundering.)

Using long strap as messenger tote. See project opener photo (page 21) for how to use the short straps to attach tote to stroller.

Burp Cloth

FINISHED BURP CLOTH: 7½″ × 21½″

Materials

Fabric A: ¼ yard for main fabric

Fabric B: 9″ × 23″ for backing

Fusible T-shirt interfacing: 9″ × 23″
(such as T-Shirt Quilt Fusible Interfacing by June Tailor, Inc.)

Assorted scraps: For paper piecing (See your selected block's materials list.)

Cutting

WOF = width of fabric

Fabric A

• Using the Burp Cloth Center pattern (page 29), cut 1 burp cloth center.

• Use remainder of fabric for paper piecing background.

Sewing

Use ¼″ seams throughout, unless otherwise directed.

PAPER-PIECED BLOCKS

Refer to Paper-Piecing Basics (page 7) as needed. Refer to Block Patterns (page 39) to choose blocks.

1 Paper piece 2 selected *square* blocks, using the assorted scraps.

2 Add any necessary embroidery.

3 Trim the blocks to 8″ × 8″.

CONSTRUCT THE FRONT OF THE BURP CLOTH

1 Sew a paper-pieced block to opposite sides of the burp cloth center. Press the seams toward the center piece.

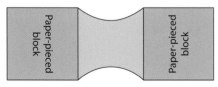

Add paper-pieced blocks to center fabric.

2 Remove the paper from the back of the paper-pieced blocks.

BURP CLOTH LINING

1 Press the fusible T-shirt interfacing to the back of the burp cloth unit, placing a sheet of paper beneath the burp cloth to prevent any excess interfacing from sticking to the iron or ironing board. Trim the excess interfacing.

2 Pin the burp cloth front to the Fabric B lining, right sides together. Stitch ¼″ from the edge of the burp cloth front, leaving a 5″ opening along the side edge of 1 paper-pieced block.

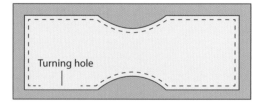

Stitch burp cloth front to lining.

3 Trim away the excess fabric. Clip the curves and corners. Turn the burp cloth right side out through the turning hole. Press. Hand stitch the 5″ opening closed. Topstitch ¼″ away from the edge.

4 Quilt over the burp cloth, through all thicknesses.

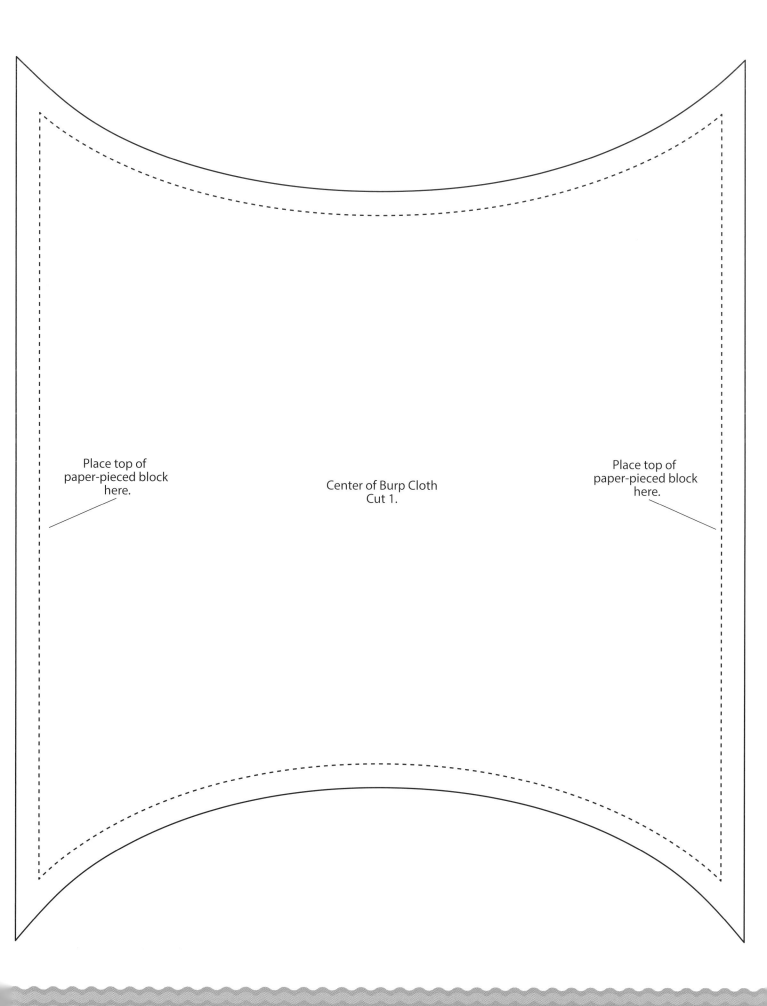

Place top of
paper-pieced block
here.

Center of Burp Cloth
Cut 1.

Place top of
paper-pieced block
here.

Catch-all

FINISHED CATCH-ALL: 9″ wide × 15″ high

Materials

Fabric A: ½ yard for main fabric

Fabric B: ⅝ yard for lining

Fabric C: 1 fat quarter for paper piecing background

One-sided fusible foam stabilizer: 1⅛ yards
(such as Bosal In-R-Form Single Sided Fusible Foam Stabilizer)

Heavyweight double-sided fusible interfacing: ¼ yard
(such as fast2fuse HEAVY Interfacing by C&T Publishing)

Assorted scraps: For paper piecing (See your selected block's materials list.)

Cutting

WOF = width of fabric

Fabric A

• Cut 1 rectangle 15½″ × 21″.

• Using the 9½″ Circle pattern (page 33), cut 1 circle.

Fabric B

Fold fabric selvage to selvage.

• Cut 1 strip 2½″ × WOF.

• Cut 1 rectangle 15½″ × 28 ½″.

• Using the 9½″ Circle pattern (page 33), cut 1 circle.

Foam stabilizer

• Cut 1 rectangle 15½″ × 28″.

• Using the 9½″ Circle pattern (page 33), cut 1 circle.

Heavyweight fusible interfacing

• Using the 9″ Circle pattern (page 34), cut 1 circle.

Sewing

Use ¼″ seams throughout, unless otherwise directed.

PAPER-PIECED BLOCKS

Refer to Paper-Piecing Basics (page 7) as needed. Refer to Block Patterns (page 39) to choose blocks.

1 Paper piece 1 selected *vertical rectangular* block, using Fabric C as the background fabric of the block and the assorted scraps for the rest of the block. Or paper piece 1 *square* block and add an 8″ × 8″ square of Fabric C to the bottom of the block.

2 Add any necessary embroidery.

3 Trim the block to 8″ × 15½″.

ASSEMBLE THE OUTSIDE OF THE CATCH-ALL

1 Sew the Fabric A rectangle to one side edge of the paper-pieced block. Press the seam open. Remove the paper from the back of the paper-pieced block. Steam press the foam stabilizer to the back of the unit, leaving a ¼″ seam allowance with no stabilizer on each 15½″ edge. (It is not necessary to catch the stabilizer in the seam, as it is fused in place.)

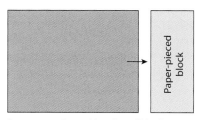

Sew rectangle to side edge of block.

2 Quilt the paper-pieced block area.

3 With right sides together, sew the side edge of the Fabric A rectangle to the side edge of the paper-pieced block, forming a tube shape. Press the seam open. *Do not turn right side out.*

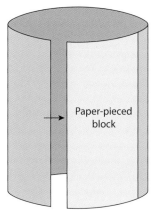

Sew into tube shape.

ATTACH THE BOTTOM

1 Fold the Fabric A 9½″ circle into quarters and press. Mark each quarter with chalk on the right side of the fabric. Steam press the 9½″ foam stabilizer circle to the wrong side of the Fabric A 9½″ circle.

2 Flatten the tube slightly, and mark the bottom edge into quarter sections with chalk.

3 Matching the quarter chalk marks, pin the circle to the bottom of the tube, placing the right sides together. Pin every 2″. Sew the seam through all layers. Turn the tube right side out.

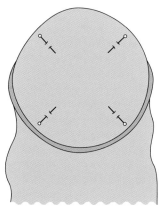

Sew circle of fabric to bottom of tube.

PREPARE THE LINING

1 Sew the 15½″ edges of Fabric B into a tube.

2 Fold the Fabric B 9½″ circle into quarters and press. Mark each quarter with chalk on the right side of the fabric. Steam press the interfacing 9″ circle to the wrong side of the lining circle, centering it on the fabric circle.

3 Flatten the lining tube slightly, and mark the bottom edge into quarter sections with chalk.

4 Matching the quarter chalk marks, pin the circle to the bottom of the lining, placing right sides together. Pin every 2″. Sew the seam. Clip curve every 1″.

BINDING

1 Slide the lining unit inside the catch-all tube, wrong sides together. Pin together along the top edge and baste ⅛″ from edge if you wish.

2 Prepare the Fabric B binding strip by folding it in half lengthwise and pressing.

3 On the outside of the tube, align the raw edges of the binding strip with the raw edges of the tube and lining. Bend the beginning of the strip on a right (90°) angle with the tail facing away from the tube.

4 Stitch ¼″ from the raw edges.

Pin binding strip to top of tube. Start stitching here.

5 Trim the end of the binding strip so it overlaps the angled beginning section by 2″, and sew in place. Trim away the remaining tail.

Overlap binding tails.

6 Press the binding around to the inside of the catch-all tube and hand stitch in place, easing in the fullness where the tails overlap.

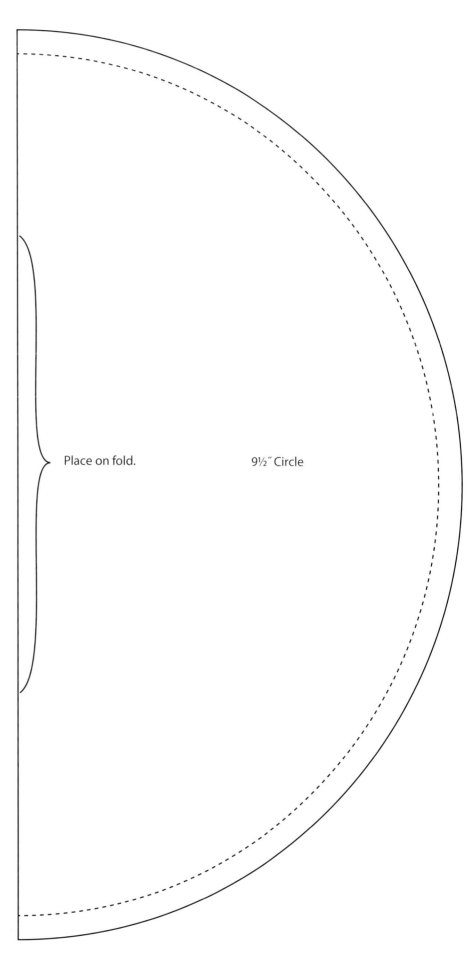

Place on fold.

9½″ Circle

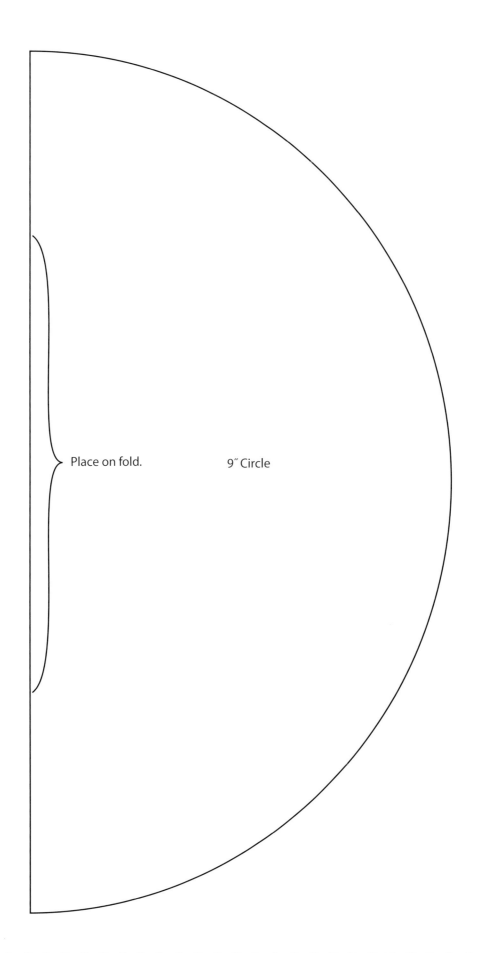

Place on fold.   9″ Circle

Baby Bib

FINISHED BIB: 9½˝ wide × 17˝ long

Materials

Fabric A: ⅓ yard for main fabric

Fabric B: 1 fat quarter for backing

Fusible T-shirt interfacing: 12″ × 19″ (such as T-Shirt Quilt Fusible Interfacing by June Tailor, Inc.)

Assorted scraps: For paper piecing (See your selected block's materials list.)

Hook-and-loop tape: 1″ × 1″ square

Cutting

WOF = width of fabric

Fabric A

• Using the Bib Top pattern (page 38), cut 1 bib top.

Fold fabric selvage to selvage for the following cutting instructions:

• Cut 1 strip 1½″ × WOF. Subcut into 2 rectangles 1½″ × 8″ and 1 rectangle 1½″ × 10″.

• Use remainder of fabric for paper piecing background.

Sewing

Use ¼″ seams throughout, unless otherwise directed.

PAPER-PIECED BLOCKS

Refer to Paper-Piecing Basics (page 7) as needed. Refer to Block Patterns (page 39) to choose a block.

1 Paper piece 1 selected square block (page 39), using the assorted scraps.

2 Add any necessary embroidery.

3 Trim the block to 8″ × 8″.

CONSTRUCT THE BIB FRONT

1 Sew the Fabric A 1½″ × 8″ strips to the sides of the paper-pieced block, right sides together. Press the seam toward Fabric A.

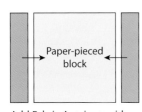

Add Fabric A strips to sides.

2 Sew the Fabric A 1½″ × 10″ to the bottom of the paper-pieced unit. Press the seam toward Fabric A.

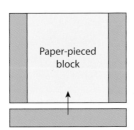

Add Fabric A strip to bottom.

3 Sew the Fabric A bib top to the top of the paper-pieced unit, right sides together. Press the seam toward the bib top.

Remove the paper from the back of the paper-pieced block.

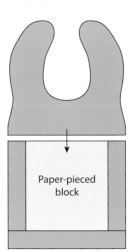

Sew bib top to block unit.

BIB LINING

1 Press the fusible T-shirt interfacing to the back of the bib front, placing a sheet of paper beneath the bib to prevent any excess interfacing from sticking to the iron or the ironing board. Trim the excess interfacing.

2 Pin the bib front to the Fabric B lining, right sides together. Stitch ¼″ from the edge of the bib front, leaving a 5″ opening along the bottom edge of the bib.

3 Trim away the excess fabric. Clip the curves. Turn the bib right side out. Press. Hand stitch the 5″ opening closed. Topstitch ¼″ away from the edge.

4 Quilt over the paper-pieced block through all thicknesses.

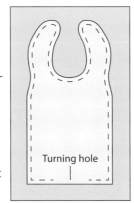

Turning hole

Stitch bib front to lining.

FINISHING

1 Stitch the male side of the 1″ × 1″ hook-and-loop tape to the lining side of the bib. Stitch the female side of the 1″ × 1″ hook-and-loop tape to the Fabric A side of the bib.

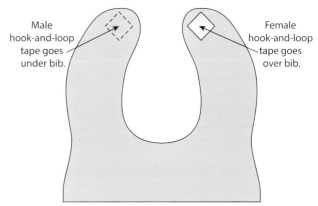

Male hook-and-loop tape goes under bib.

Female hook-and-loop tape goes over bib.

Sew hook-and-loop tape to bib.

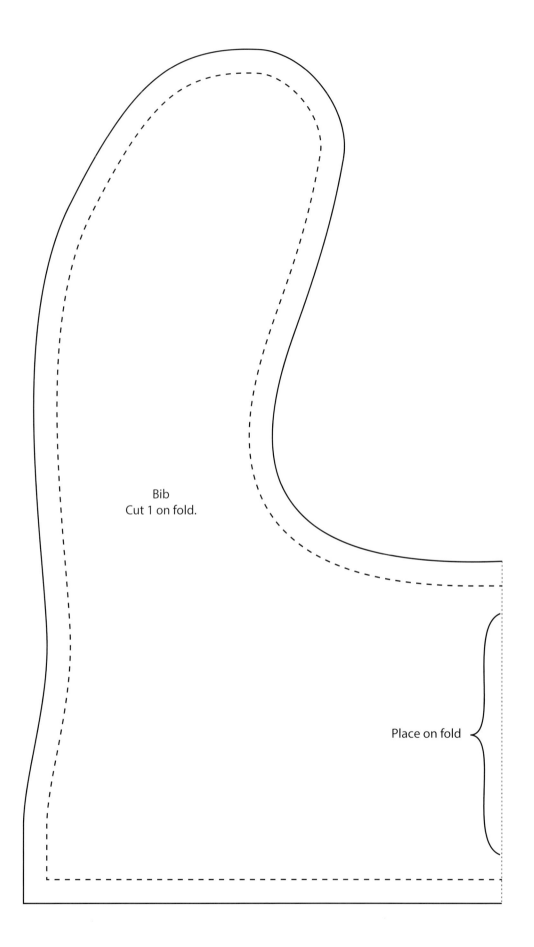

Bib
Cut 1 on fold.

Place on fold

Block Patterns

- When making the blocks, refer to Paper-Piecing Basics (page 7) as needed.

- Refer to the specific project instructions about when to remove foundation papers. Any hand embroidery included in the following block instructions is meant to be done with foundation papers attached. (I use a running stitch or make French knots, page 16, with 6 strands embroidery floss.)

- The first fabric in the materials list is for the block background. If your project includes background fabric in its materials list, you can ignore the requirement listed for the block.

- *For baby's safety:* The projects in this book are intended for babies, so, for safety reasons, no buttons or other embellishments besides embroidery floss have been used in the instructions. If you wish to embellish the projects further than in the instructions, use thread or floss only. Be sure *not* to use any buttons or embellishments that could present a choking hazard.

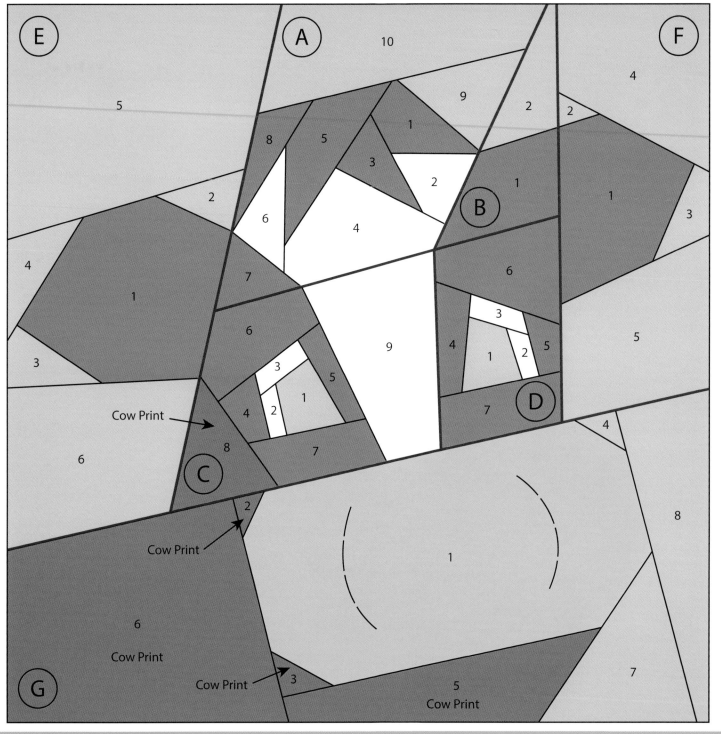

E
A
10
F
5
9
1
8
5
3
2
2
4
6
2
4
4
7
B
1
1
6
3
4
1
6
3
9
4
5
1
2
5
Cow Print
3
5
5
4
2
1
D
8
4
7
C
7
2
Cow Print
8
6
4
6
1
Cow Print
G
6
8
Cow Print
3
Cow Print
5
7
Cow Print

CALF

Materials
- Large scrap of blue, at least 9″ × 11″
- Scraps of white, black, turquoise, pink, and white with black spots
- Black embroidery floss

Directions
For detailed directions, refer to Paper-Piecing Basics (page 7).

1. Make 4 copies of the pattern (A/G, B/E, C/F, D).
2. Cut around each segment, adding ¼″ seam allowances.
3. Paper piece each segment.
4. Connect the segments: A to B; C to D; A/B to C/D; A/B/C/D to E to F; A–F to G.
5. Trim the block to 8″ × 8″.
6. Hand stitch the nostrils and pupils with black embroidery floss.

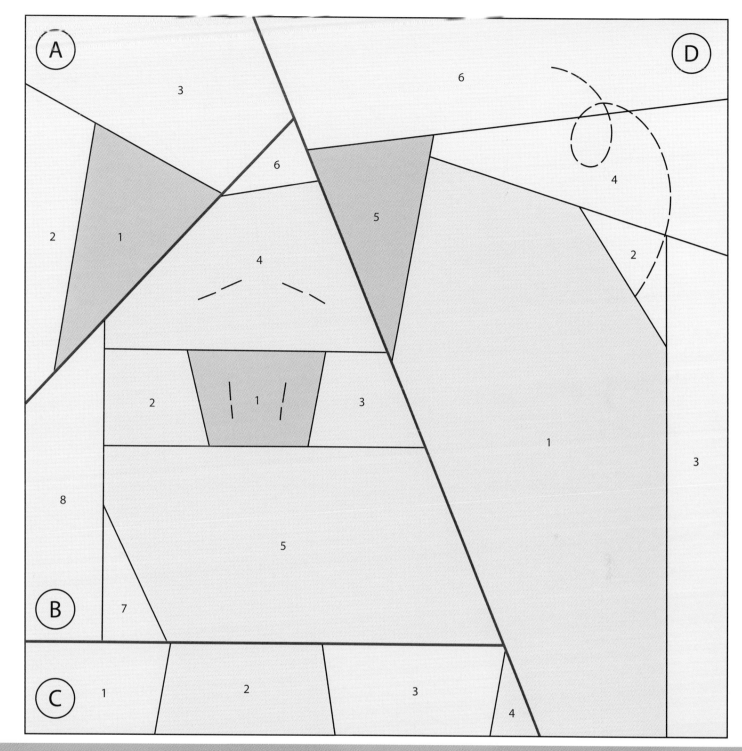

PIGLET

Materials

- Large scrap of blue, at least 9″ × 11″
- Scraps of light pink and dark pink
- Black embroidery floss

Directions

For detailed directions, refer to Paper-Piecing Basics (page 7).

1. Make 3 copies of the pattern (A/C, B, D).

2. Cut around each segment, adding ¼″ seam allowances.

3. Paper piece each segment.

4. Connect the segments: A to B to C; A/B/C to D.

5. Trim the block to 8″ × 8″.

6. Hand stitch the eyes, nostrils, and tail using black embroidery floss.

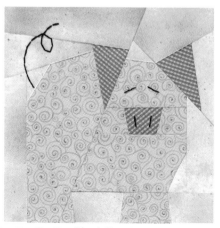

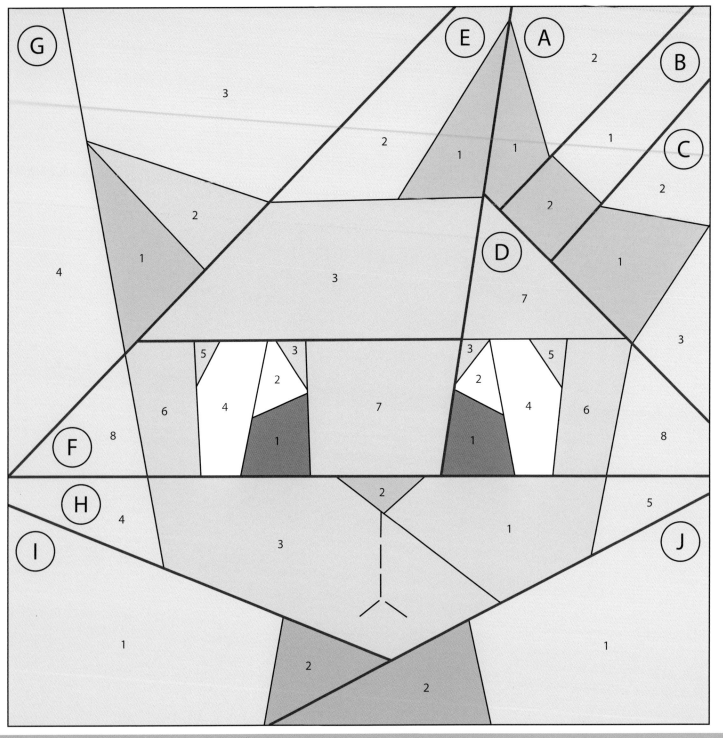

KITTEN

Materials

- Large scrap of blue, at least 12″ × 12″
- Scraps of black, white, light pink, dark pink, light gray, and dark gray
- Black embroidery floss

Directions

For detailed directions, refer to Paper-Piecing Basics (page 7).

1. Make 4 copies of the pattern (A/C/F, B/G/J, D/I, E/H).

2. Cut around each segment, adding ¼″ seam allowances.

3. Paper piece each segment.

4. Connect the segments: A to B to C; A/B/C to D; E to F; A/B/C/D to E/F to G; H to I to J; A–G to H/I/J.

5. Trim the block to 8″ × 8″.

6. Hand stitch the mouth using black embroidery floss.

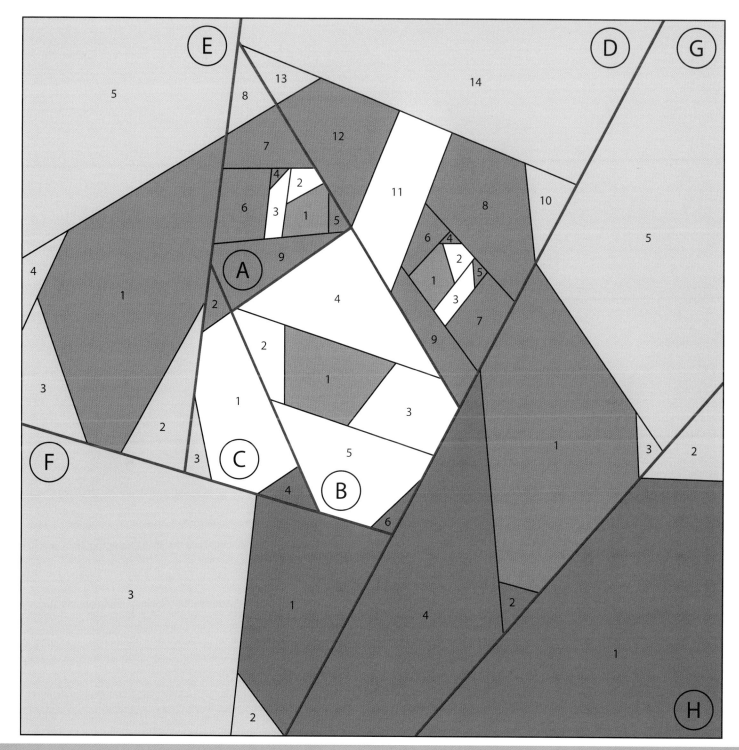

PUPPY

Materials

- Large scrap of blue, at least 10″ × 12″
- Scraps of white, light brown, dark brown, and black

Directions

For detailed directions, refer to Paper-Piecing Basics (page 7).

1. Make 4 copies of the pattern (A/F/H, B/E, C/D, G).

2. Cut around each segment, adding ¼″ seam allowances.

3. Paper piece each segment.

4. Connect the segments: A to B; A/B to C; A/B/C to D; A–D to E to F; A–F to G to H.

5. Trim the block to 8″ × 8″.

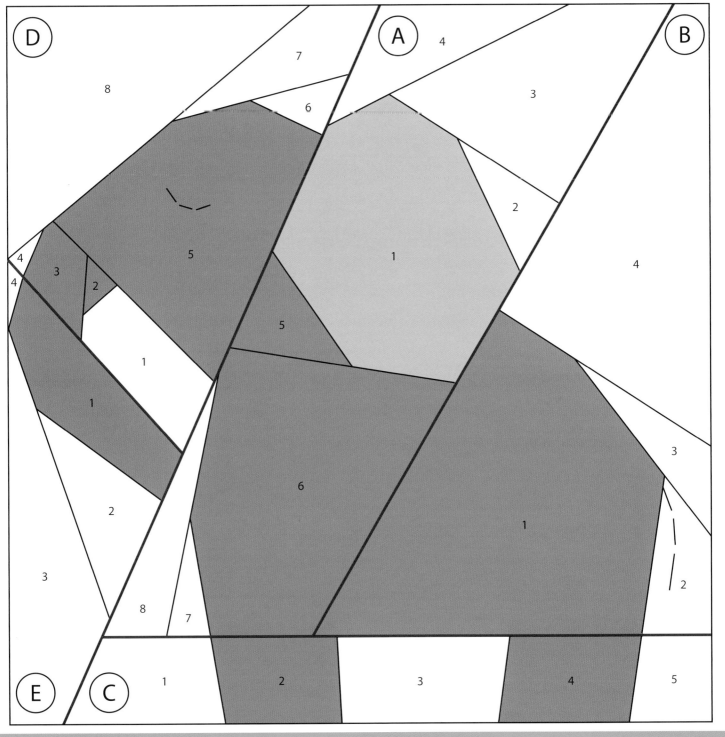

BABY ELEPHANT

Materials

- Large scrap of white with print, at least 12″ × 15″
- Scraps of gray and pink
- Black embroidery floss

Directions

For detailed directions, refer to Paper-Piecing Basics (page 7).

1. Make 3 copies of the pattern (A, B/E, C/D).

2. Cut around each segment, adding ¼″ seam allowances.

3. Paper piece each segment.

4. Connect the segments: A to B; A/B to C; D to E; A/B/C to D/E.

5. Trim the block to 8″ × 8″.

6. Hand stitch the eye and tail using black embroidery floss.

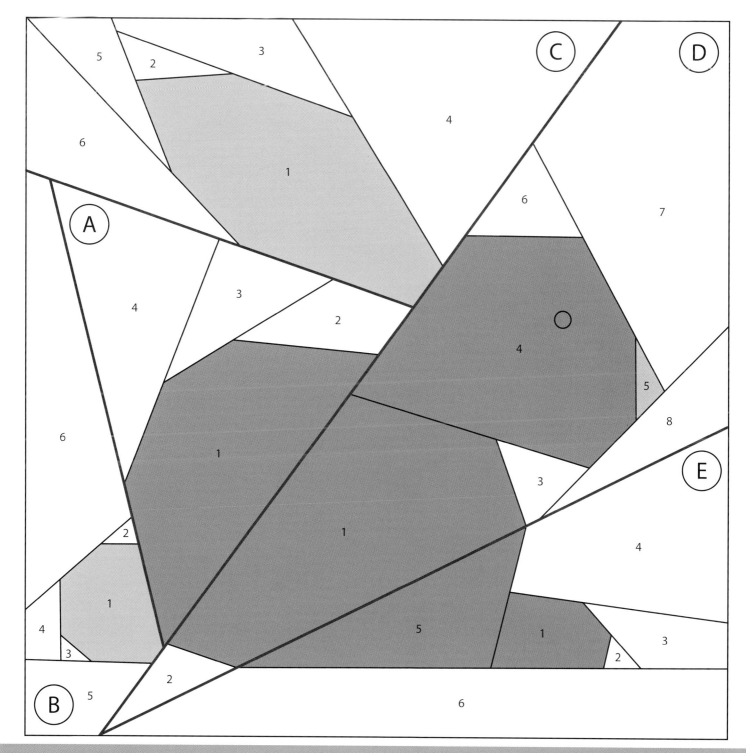

BUNNY

Materials

- Large scrap of white with print, at least 12″ × 15″
- Scraps of gray and pink
- Black embroidery floss

Directions

For detailed directions, refer to Paper-Piecing Basics (page 7).

1. Make 4 copies of the pattern (A/E, B, C, D).

2. Cut around each segment, adding ¼″ seam allowances.

3. Paper piece each segment.

4. Connect the segments: A to B; A/B to C; A/B/C to D to E.

5. Trim the block to 8″ × 8″.

6. Hand stitch the eye by filling in the circle with a satin stitch, using black embroidery floss.

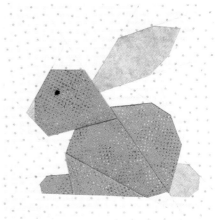

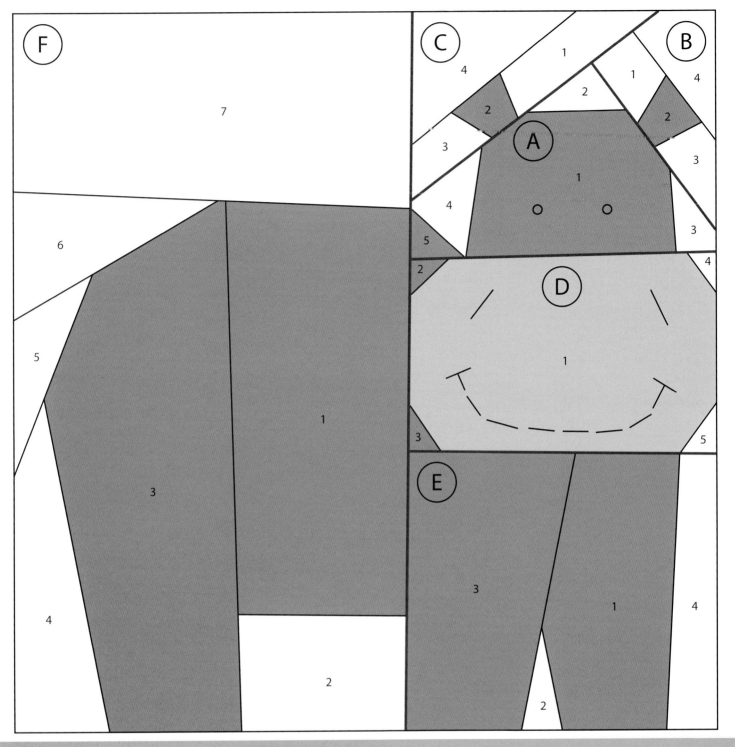

BABY HIPPO

Materials

- Large scrap of white with print, at least 9″ × 11″
- Scraps of gray and pink
- Black embroidery floss

Directions

For detailed directions, refer to Paper-Piecing Basics (page 7).

1. Make 3 copies of the pattern (A/E, B/F, C/D).

2. Cut around each segment, adding ¼″ seam allowances.

3. Paper piece each segment.

4. Connect the segments: A to B; A/B to C; A/B/C to D to E; A–E to F.

5. Trim the block to 8″ × 8″.

6. Using black embroidery floss, hand stitch the nostrils and mouth, and embroider French knots (page 16) for the eyes.

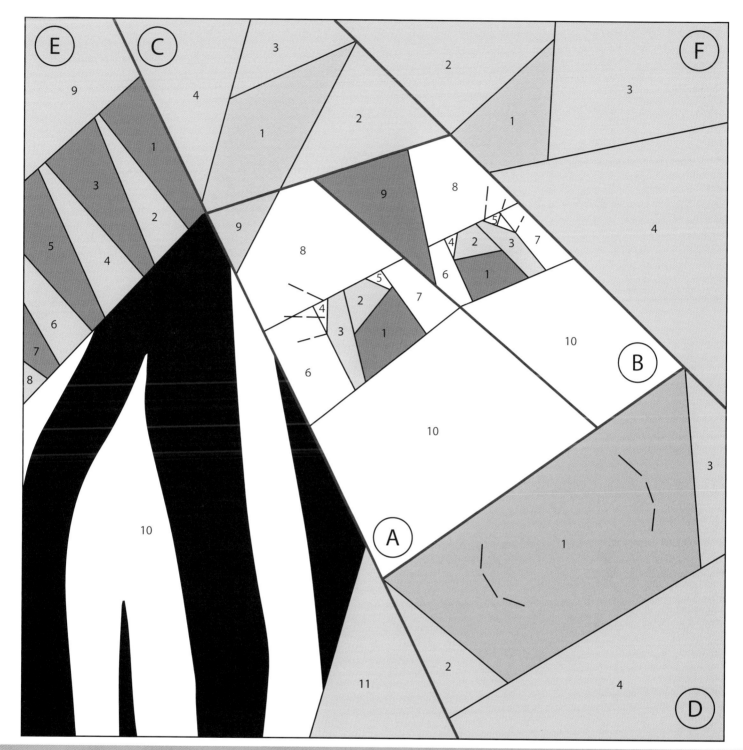

BABY ZEBRA

Materials

- Large scrap of blue, at least 12″ × 15″
- Scraps of white, black, pink, turquoise, gray, and black-and-white stripe
- Black embroidery floss

Directions

For detailed directions, refer to Paper-Piecing Basics (page 7).

1. Make 3 copies of the pattern (A/F, B/E, C/D).

2. Cut around each segment, adding ¼″ seam allowances.

3. Paper piece each segment.

4. Connect the segments: A to B; A/B to C to D; A–D to E to F.

5. Trim the block to 8″ × 8″.

6. Hand stitch the eyelashes and nostrils using black embroidery floss.

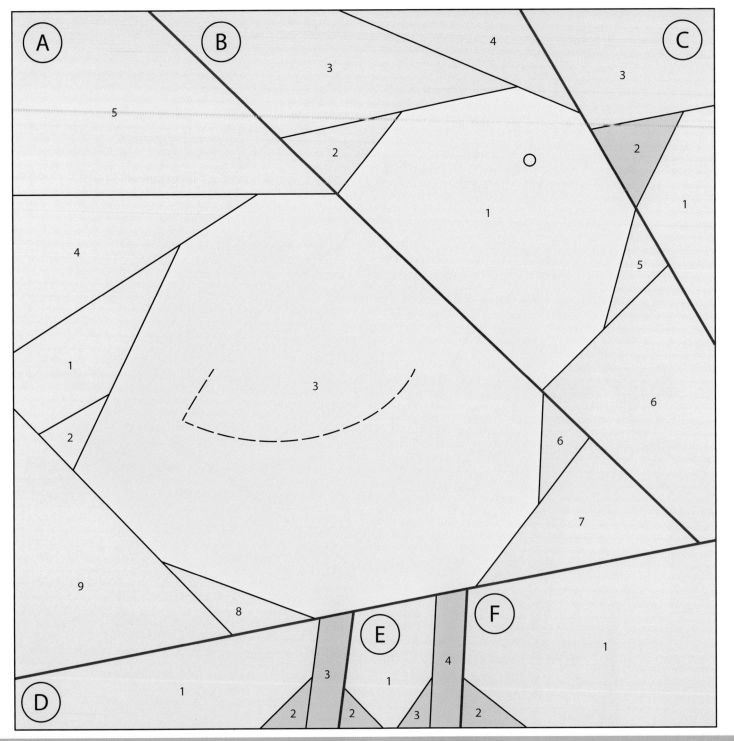

A

B

3

4

C

5

2

3

2

O

1

1

4

5

1

3

2

6

6

7

9

8

E

F

1

3

1

4

D

1

2

2

3

2

CHICK

Materials

- Large scrap of blue, at least 12″ × 15″
- Scraps of orange and yellow
- Black embroidery floss

Directions

For detailed directions, refer to Paper-Piecing Basics (page 7).

1. Make 3 copies of the pattern (A/C, D/F, B/E).

2. Cut around each segment, adding ¼″ seam allowances.

3. Paper piece each segment.

4. Connect the segments: A to B to C; D to E to F; A/B/C to D/E/F.

5. Trim the block to 8″ × 8″.

6. Using black embroidery floss, hand stitch the wing using black embroidery floss, and fill the eye circle with satin stitches.

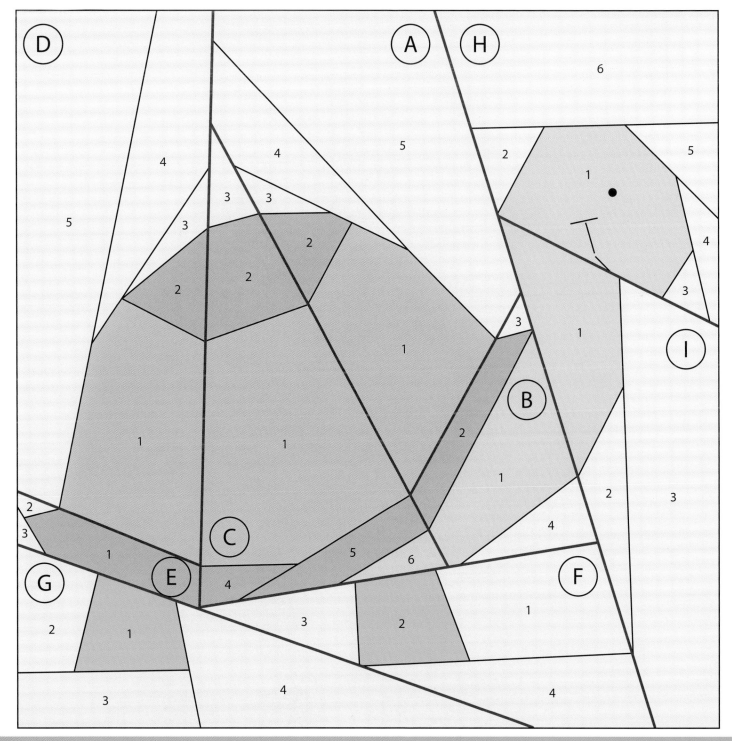

TURTLE HATCHLING

Materials

- Large scrap of blue, at least 12″ × 15″
- Scraps of orange, orange print, light green, and dark green
- Black embroidery floss

Directions

For detailed directions, refer to Paper-Piecing Basics (page 7).

1. Make 4 copies of the pattern (A/F, B/D/G, C/H, E/I).

2. Cut around each segment, adding ¼″ seam allowances.

3. Paper piece each segment.

4. Connect the segments: A to B; A/B to C; D to E; A/B/C to D/E to F to G; H to I; A–G to H/I.

5. Trim the block to 8″ × 8″.

6. Using black embroidery floss, hand stitch the mouth, and stitch a French knot (page 16) for the eye.

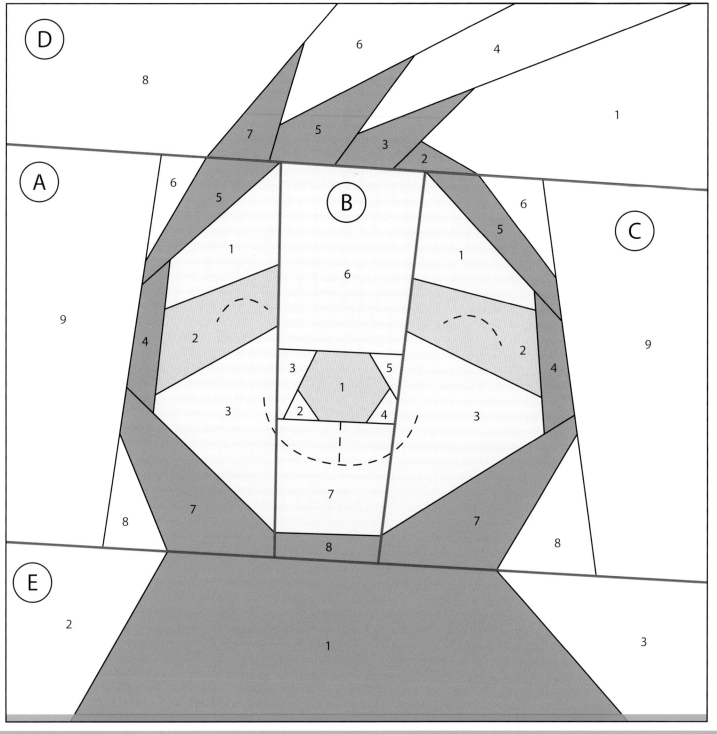

BABY SLOTH, PART 1

Materials
- Large scrap of gray, at least 12″ × 15″
- Scraps of cream, light brown, medium brown, and black
- Black embroidery floss

Directions
For detailed directions, refer to Paper-Piecing Basics (page 7).

1. Make 3 copies of the pattern (A/C, B, D/E).

2. Cut around each segment, adding ¼″ seam allowances.

3. Paper piece each segment.

4. Connect the segments: A to B to C; A/B/C to D to E.

5. Trim ¼″ from the blue line.

6. Stitch the eyes and mouth using black embroidery floss.

7. Continue to Baby Sloth, Part 2 (next page).

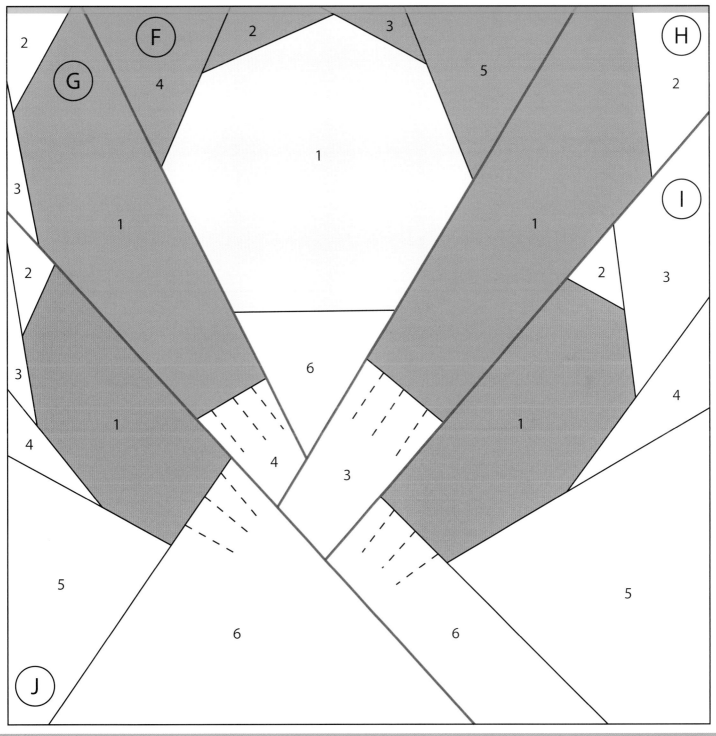

BABY SLOTH, PART 2

Materials

- Large scrap of gray, at least 12″ × 15″
- Scraps of cream, medium brown, and dark brown
- Black embroidery floss

Directions

For detailed directions, refer to Paper-Piecing Basics (page 7).

1. Make 3 copies of the pattern (F/J, G/I, H).

2. Cut around each segment, adding ¼″ seam allowances.

3. Paper piece each segment.

4. Connect the segments: F to G; F/G to H to I; F–I to J.

5. Trim ¼″ from the blue line. Match and sew Part 1 to Part 2 on the blue lines.

6. Trim the block to 8″ × 15½″.

7. Hand stitch the toes using black embroidery floss.

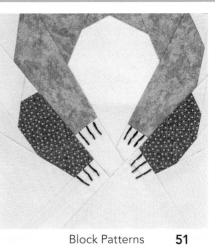

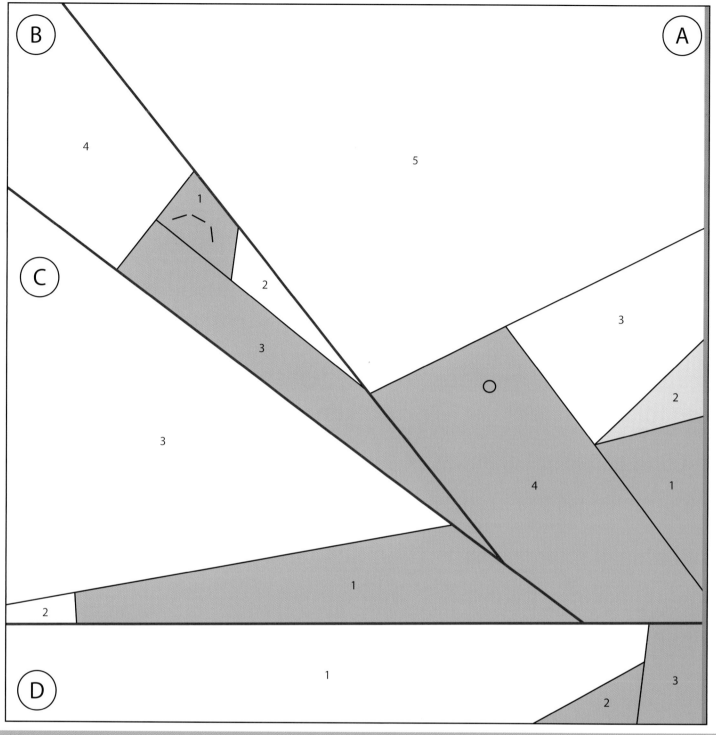

BABY ALLIGATOR, PART 1

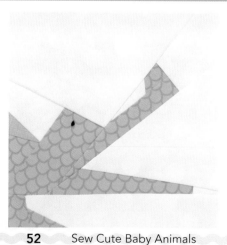

Materials

- Large scrap of white, at least 9″ × 11″
- Scraps of light green and medium green
- Black embroidery floss

Directions

For detailed directions, refer to Paper-Piecing Basics (page 7).

1. Make 3 copies of the pattern (A, B/D, C).

2. Cut around each segment, adding ¼″ seam allowances.

3. Paper piece each segment.

4. Connect the segments: A to B; A/B to C; A/B/C to D.

5. Trim ¼″ from the blue line.

6. Hand stitch the nostril and the eye with French knots (page 16) using black embroidery floss.

7. Continue to Baby Alligator, Part 2 (next page).

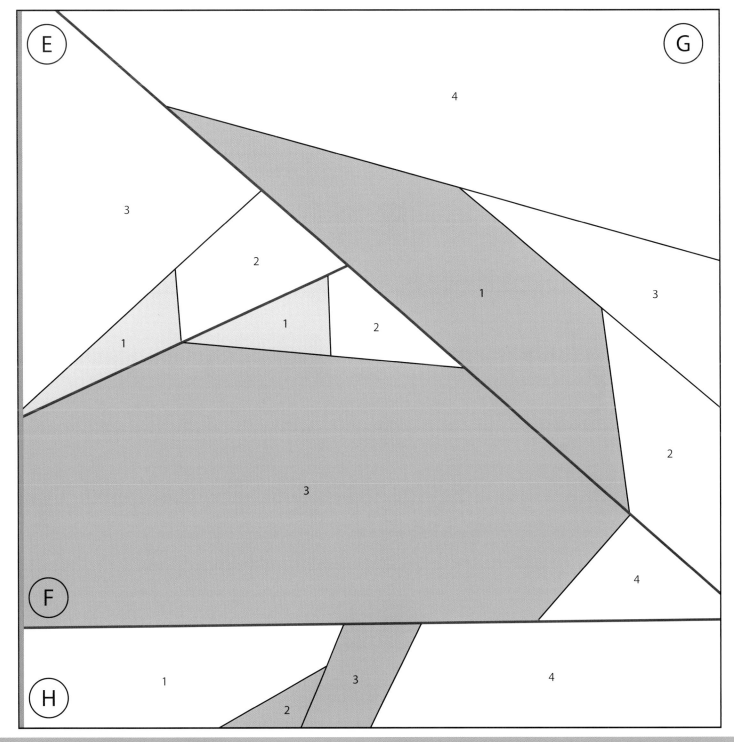

BABY ALLIGATOR, PART 2

Materials
- Large scrap of white, at least 9″ × 11″
- Scraps of light green and green

Directions
For detailed directions, refer to Paper-Piecing Basics (page 7).

1. Make 3 copies of the pattern (E/H, F, G).

2. Cut around each segment, adding ¼″ seam allowances.

3. Paper piece each segment.

4. Connect the segments: E to F to G; E/F/G to H.

5. Trim ¼″ from the blue line. Match and sew Part 1 to Part 2 on the blue lines.

6. Trim the block to 8″ × 15½″.

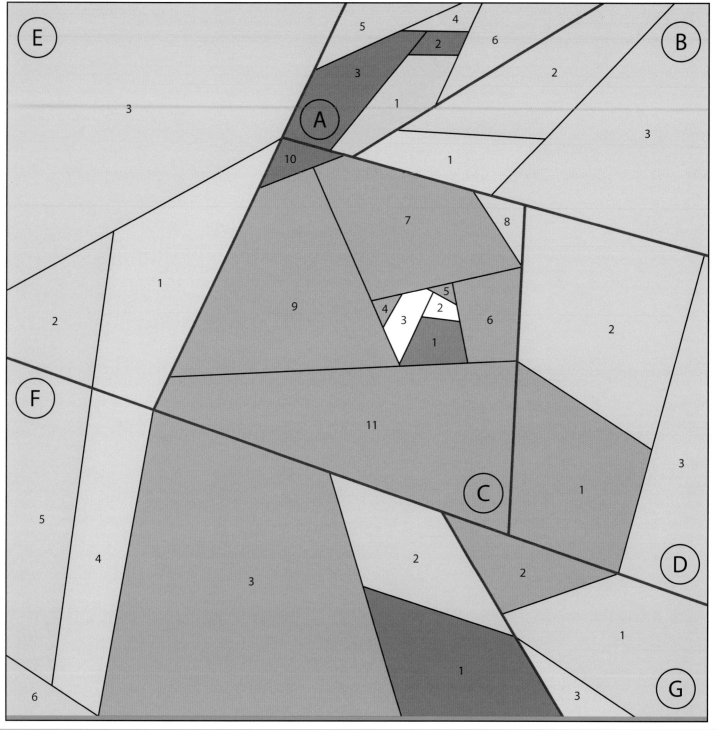

FOAL, PART 1

Materials

- Large scrap of blue, at least 12" × 15"
- Scraps of black, white, light brown, dark brown, pink, and white-and-brown stripe

Directions

For detailed directions, refer to Paper-Piecing Basics (page 7).

1. Make 3 copies of the pattern (A/D/F, B/E/G, C).

2. Cut around each segment, adding ¼" seam allowances.

3. Paper piece each segment.

4. Connect the segments: A to B; C to D; A/B to C/D; A/B/C/D to E; F to G; A–E to F/G.

5. Trim ¼" from the blue line.

6. Continue to Foal, Part 2 (next page).

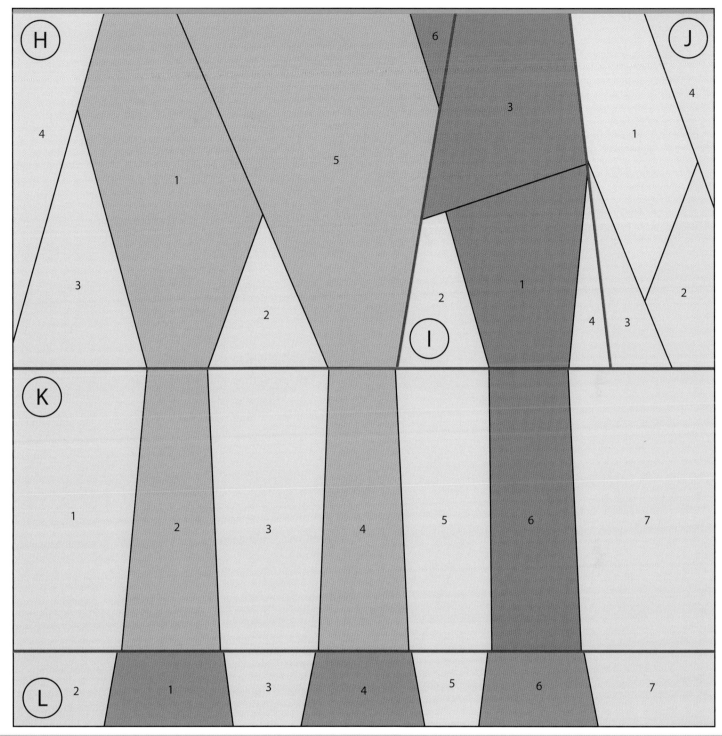

FOAL, PART 2

Materials

- Large scrap of blue, at least 12″ × 15″
- Scraps of light brown, dark brown, black, and brown-and-white stripe

Directions

For detailed directions, refer to Paper-Piecing Basics (page 7).

1. Make 3 copies of the pattern (H/J/L, I, K).

2. Cut around each segment, adding ¼″ seam allowances.

3. Paper piece each segment.

4. Connect the segments: H to I to J; H/I/J to K to L.

5. Trim ¼″ from the blue line. Match and sew Part 1 to Part 2 on the blue lines.

6. Trim the block to 8″ × 15½″.

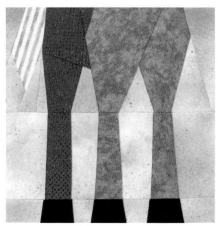

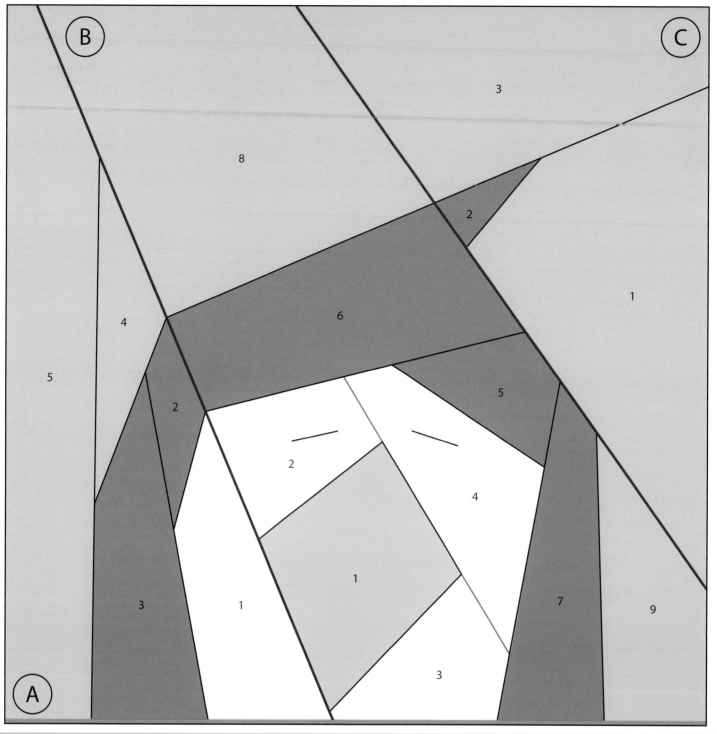

BABY PENGUIN, PART 1

Materials

- Large scrap of blue, at least 9″ × 11″
- Scraps of black, white, and orange
- Black embroidery floss

Directions

For detailed directions, refer to Paper-Piecing Basics (page 7).

1. Make 2 copies of the pattern (A/C, B).

2. Cut around each segment, adding ¼″ seam allowances.

3. Paper piece each segment.

4. Connect the segments: A to B to C.

5. Trim ¼″ from the blue line.

6. Hand stitch the eyes using black embroidery floss.

7. Continue to Baby Penguin, Part 2 (next page).

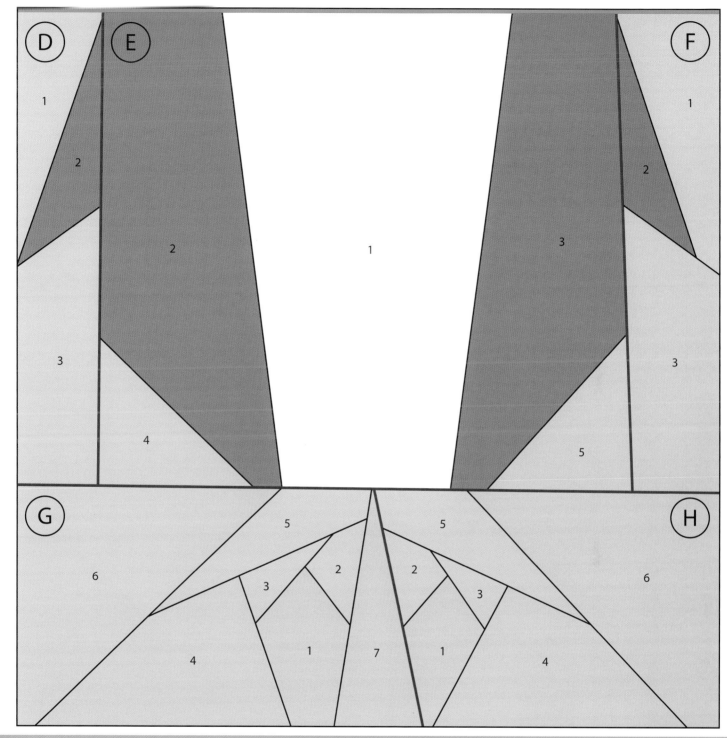

BABY PENGUIN, PART 2

Materials
- Large scrap of blue, at least 9″ × 11″
- Scraps of white, black, and orange

Directions
For detailed directions, refer to Paper-Piecing Basics (page 7).

1. Make 3 copies of the pattern (D/H, E, F/G).

2. Cut around each segment, adding ¼″ seam allowances.

3. Paper piece each segment.

4. Connect the segments: D to E to F; G to H; D/E/F to G/H.

5. Trim ¼″ from the blue line. Match and sew Part 1 to Part 2 on the blue lines.

6. Trim the block to 8″ × 15½″.

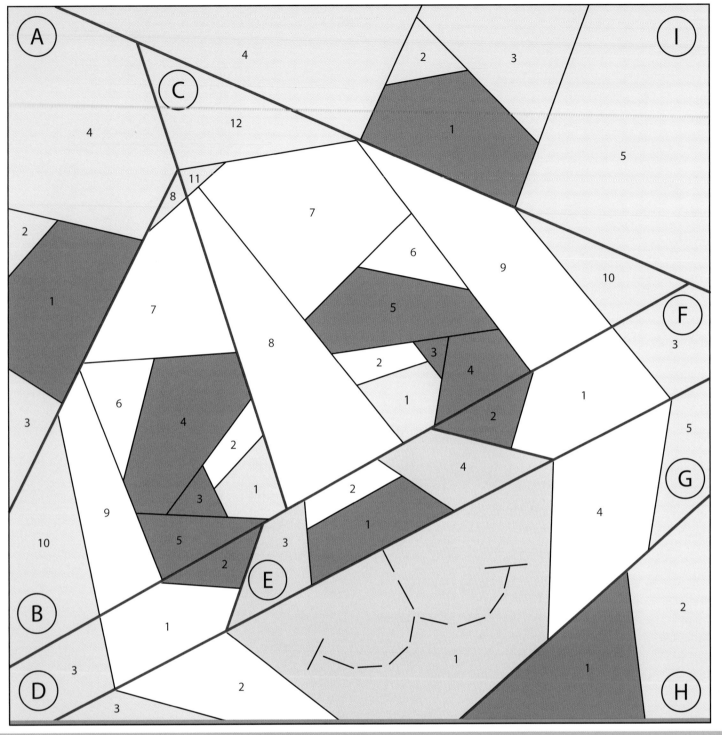

A C I
4
2 3
12
4
11
8
7
2
6
9
1 7 5
8
2 3
9
5 4
2 1 F
3
6 1 2 3
4 1
2 4
3 2 4 5
9
2 4 G
10 5 1
2 3 E
1 2 1
B 4
2
1 2
D 1 H
3 1
3 2

PANDA CUB, PART 1

Materials

- Large scrap of blue, at least 9″ × 11″
- Scraps of black, white, light gray, and turquoise
- Black embroidery floss

Directions

For detailed directions, refer to Paper-Piecing Basics (page 7).

1. Make 4 copies of the pattern (A/E, B/F/H, C/D, G/I).

2. Cut around each segment, adding ¼″ seam allowances.

3. Paper piece each segment.

4. Connect the segments: A to B; A/B/to C; D to E to F; A/B/C to D/E/F; A–F to G to H; A–H to I.

5. Trim ¼″ from the blue line.

6. Hand stitch the mouth using black embroidery floss.

7. Continue to Panda Cub, Part 2 (next page).

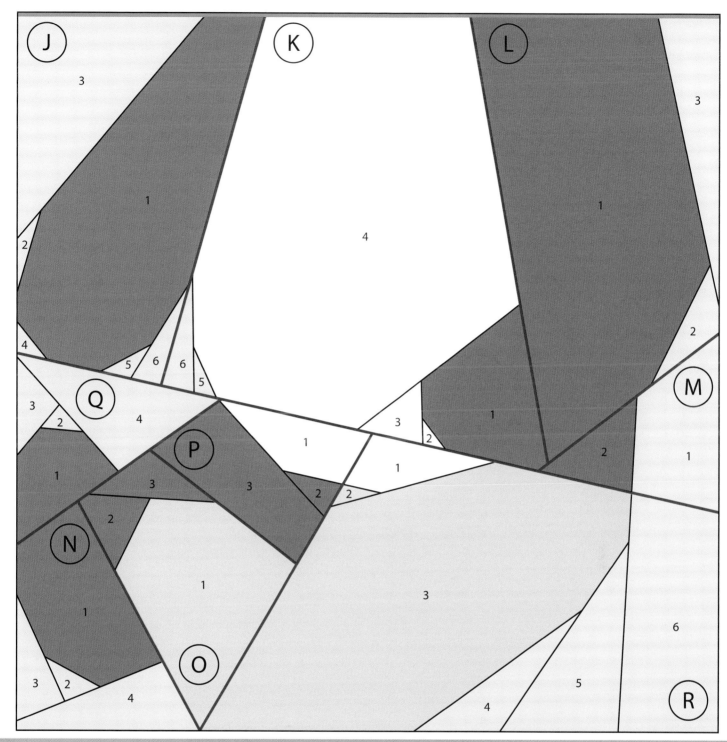

PANDA CUB, PART 2

Materials
- Large scrap of blue, at least 9″ × 11″
- Scraps of black, white, and dark gray

Directions
For detailed directions, refer to Paper-Piecing Basics (page 7).

1. Make 4 copies of the pattern (J/L/P/N, K/O, M/Q, R).

2. Cut around each segment, adding ¼″ seam allowances.

3. Paper piece each segment.

4. Connect the segments: J to K to L to M; N to O to P; N/O/P to Q; N-Q to R; J–M to N–R.

5. Trim ¼″ from the blue line. Match and sew Part 1 to Part 2 on the blue lines.

6. Trim the block to 8″ × 15½″.

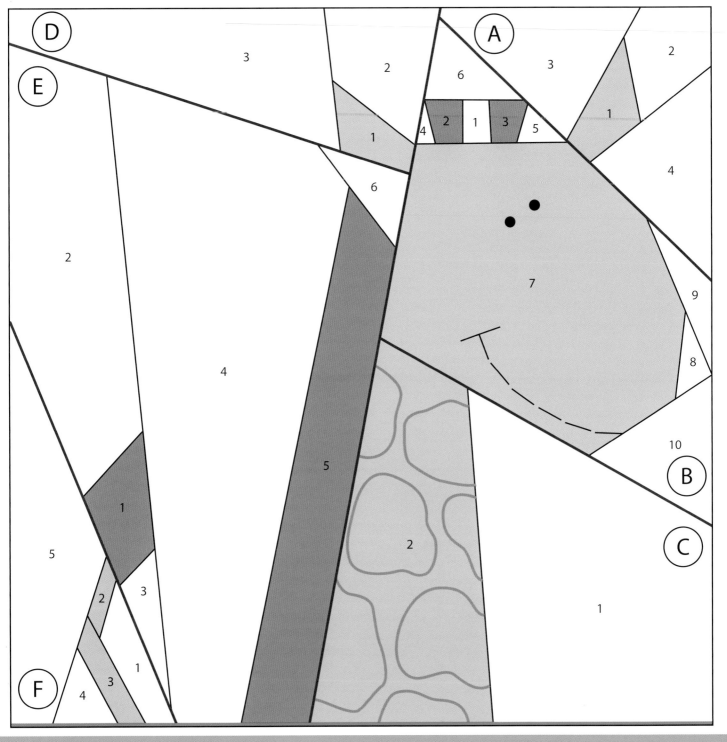

BABY GIRAFFE, PART 1

Materials

- Large scrap of white, at least 12″ × 15″
- Scraps of tan, medium brown, and tan with brown dots
- Black embroidery floss

Directions

For detailed directions, refer to Paper-Piecing Basics (page 7).

1. Make 4 copies of the pattern (A/C/F, B, D, E).

2. Cut around each segment, adding ¼″ seam allowances.

3. Paper piece each segment.

4. Connect the segments: A to B to C; D to E to F; A/B/C to D/E/F.

5. Trim ¼″ from the blue line.

6. Using black embroidery floss, hand stitch the mouth, and embroider French knots (page 16) for the eyes.

7. Continue to Baby Giraffe, Part 2 (next page).

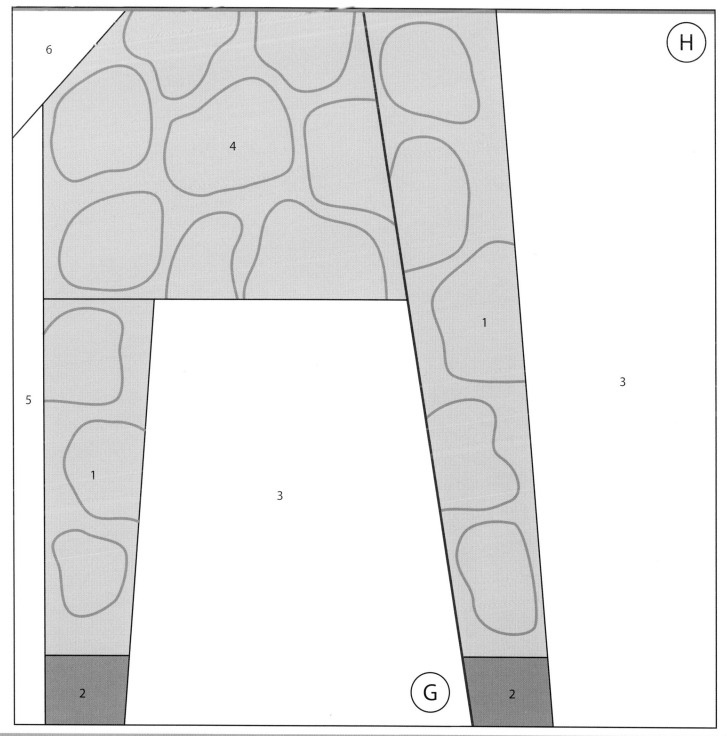

BABY GIRAFFE, PART 2

Materials

- Large scrap of white, at least 9″ × 11″
- Scraps of medium brown, and tan with brown dots

Directions

For detailed directions, refer to Paper-Piecing Basics (page 7).

1. Make 2 copies of the pattern (G, H).

2. Cut around each segment, adding ¼″ seam allowances.

3. Paper piece each segment.

4. Connect the segments: G to H.

5. Trim ¼″ from the blue line. Match and sew Part 1 to Part 2 on the blue lines.

6. Trim the block to 8″ × 15½″.

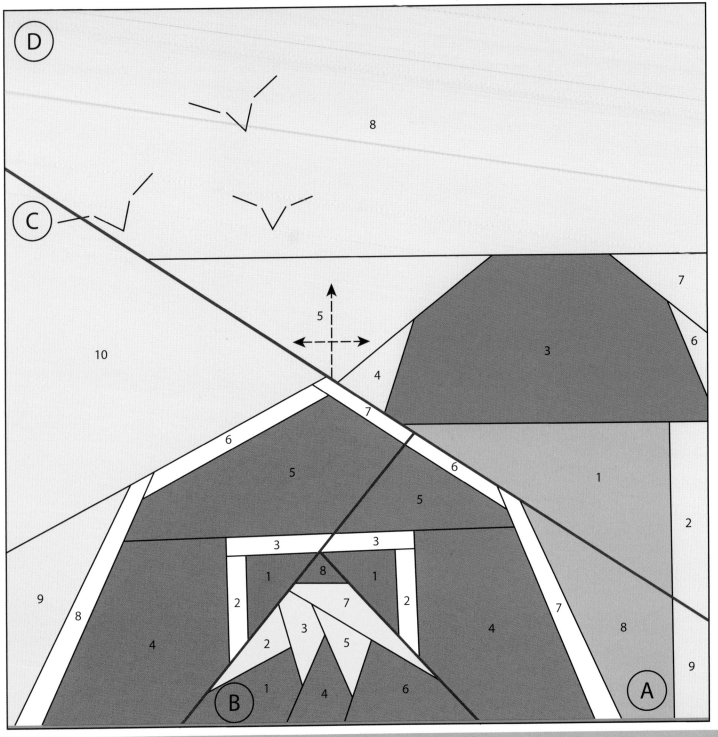

BARN, PART 1

Materials
- Large scrap of blue, at least 9″ × 11″
- Scraps of black, gray, white, red, and gold
- Black embroidery floss

Directions
For detailed directions, refer to Paper-Piecing Basics (page 7).

1. Make 3 copies of the pattern (A, B/D, C).

2. Cut around each segment, adding ¼″ seam allowances.

3. Paper piece each segment.

4. Connect the segments: A to B; A/B to C; A/B/C to D.

5. Trim ¼″ from the blue line.

6. Hand stitch the weather vane and birds using black embroidery floss.

7. Continue to Barn, Part 2 (next page).

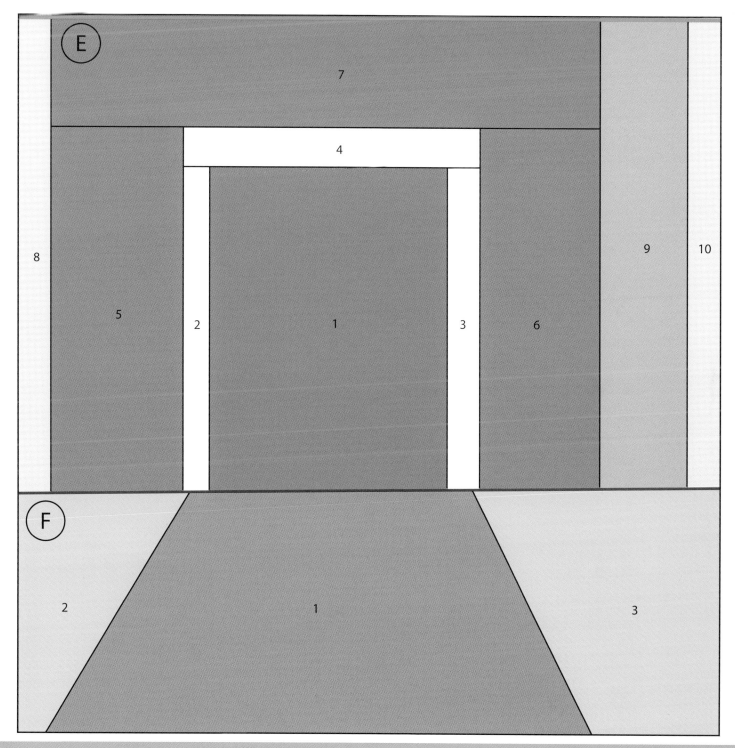

BARN, PART 2

Materials
• Scraps of blue, gray, black, white, red, brown, and green

Directions
For detailed directions, refer to Paper-Piecing Basics (page 7).

1. Make 2 copies of the pattern (E, F).

2. Cut around each segment, adding ¼″ seam allowances.

3. Paper piece each segment.

4. Connect the segments: E to F.

5. Trim ¼″ from the blue line. Match and sew Part 1 to Part 2 on the blue lines.

6. Trim the block to 8″ × 15½″.

About the Author

Mary (also known as Marney) **Hertel** grew up on a small dairy farm in the heart of Wisconsin. Sewing is in her blood, and she likes to say she has "sewn since birth," starting on her mother's sewing machine at a very early age. After securing her art education job straight out of college, she used her first paycheck to purchase a sewing machine. Soon after, she started to quilt and has never stopped.

Mary's favorite method of quilting became paper piecing after she was introduced to this practice in 2013. The puzzle-like quality of paper piecing appealed to Mary and has quickly become her favorite approach to adding an image to a quilt.

Her quirky animal designs are a nod to 35 years of teaching children's art. "I try to keep my animal designs childlike, but expressive," Mary says. She also strives to offer her customers very easy paper-pieced patterns.

Currently, Mary has five previously published books, scores of magazine articles, and more than 400 patterns that can be found on Etsy.com and in many quilting stores throughout the United States.

Enjoy her whimsical designs and her easy-to-paper-piece patterns.

Photo by Gail Cameron

Also by Mary Hertel:

Visit Mary online and follow on social media!

Website: madebymarney.com

Facebook: /madebymarney

Pinterest: /maryhertel

Instagram: @madebymarney

Twitter: @madebymarney

Etsy: etsy.com/shop/madebymarney